SMILE PLEASE, ANDY CAPP

by

Smythe

FAWCETT GOLD MEDAL • NEW YORK

SMILE PLEASE, ANDY CAPP

ANDY CAPP of the Daily Mirror, London
© 1976 Daily Mirror Newspapers Ltd.
© 1979 Daily Mirror Newspapers Ltd.

Published by Fawcett Gold Medal Books, CBS Educational and Professional Publishing, a division of CBS Inc., by special arrangement with Field Newspaper Syndicate.

All inquiries should be addressed to Hall House, Inc., 262 Mason Street, Greenwich, Connecticut.

ISBN: 0-449-14249-3

Printed in the United States of America

First Fawcett Gold Medal printing: August 1979

14   13   12   11   10   9   8   7   6   5   4

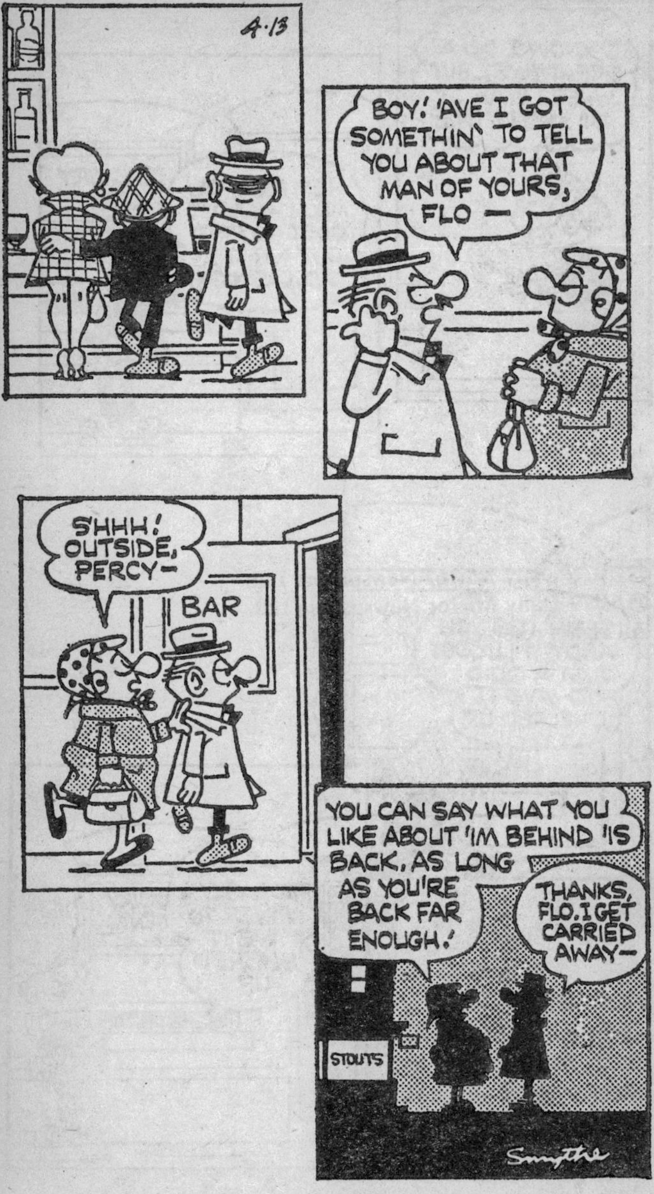
4·13
BOY! 'AVE I GOT SOMETHIN' TO TELL YOU ABOUT THAT MAN OF YOURS, FLO —
S'HHH! OUTSIDE, PERCY—
BAR
YOU CAN SAY WHAT YOU LIKE ABOUT 'IM BEHIND 'IS BACK, AS LONG AS YOU'RE BACK FAR ENOUGH!
THANKS, FLO. I GET CARRIED AWAY—
STOUTS
Smythe

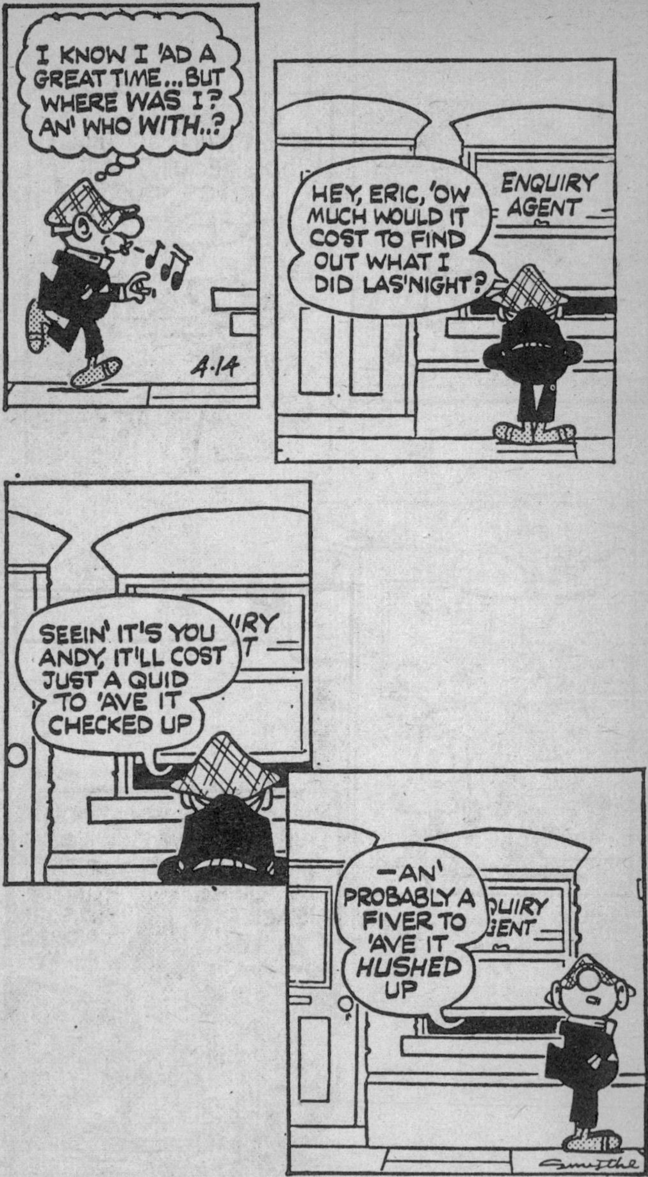
I KNOW I 'AD A GREAT TIME... BUT WHERE WAS I? AN' WHO WITH..?
4·14
ENQUIRY AGENT
HEY, ERIC, 'OW MUCH WOULD IT COST TO FIND OUT WHAT I DID LAS'NIGHT?
SEEIN' IT'S YOU ANDY, IT'LL COST JUST A QUID TO 'AVE IT CHECKED UP
—AN' PROBABLY A FIVER TO 'AVE IT HUSHED UP
Smythe

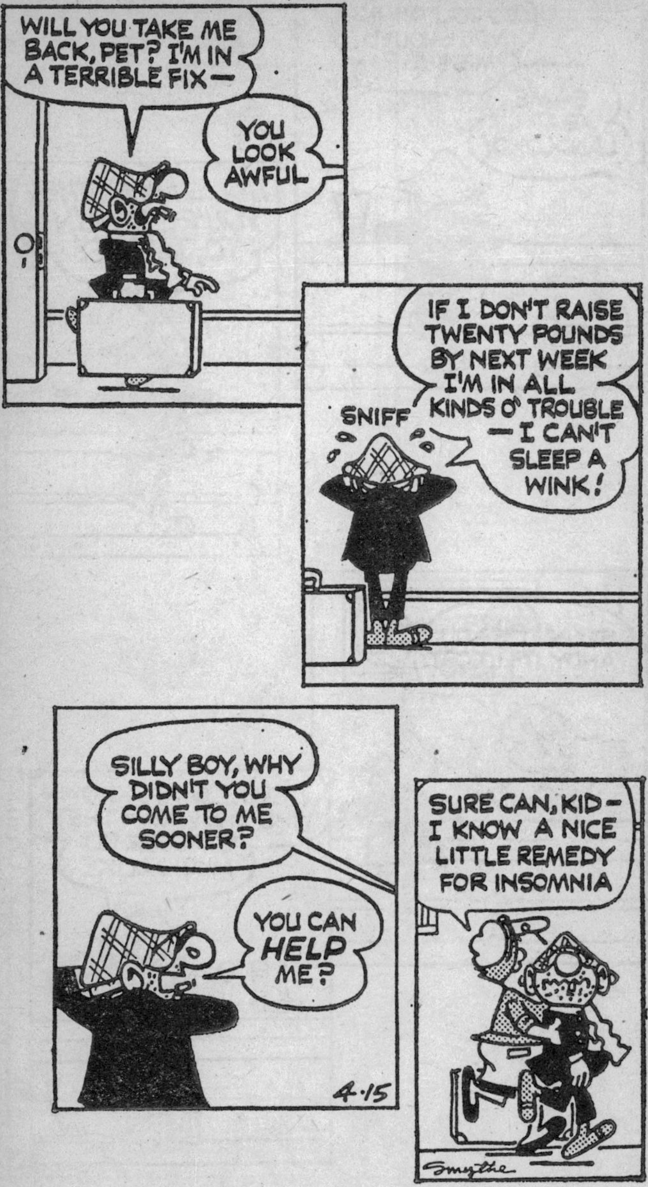
WILL YOU TAKE ME BACK, PET? I'M IN A TERRIBLE FIX—
YOU LOOK AWFUL
IF I DON'T RAISE TWENTY POUNDS BY NEXT WEEK I'M IN ALL KINDS O' TROUBLE —I CAN'T SLEEP A WINK!
SNIFF
SILLY BOY, WHY DIDN'T YOU COME TO ME SOONER?
YOU CAN *HELP* ME?
4·15
SURE CAN, KID— I KNOW A NICE LITTLE REMEDY FOR INSOMNIA
Smythe

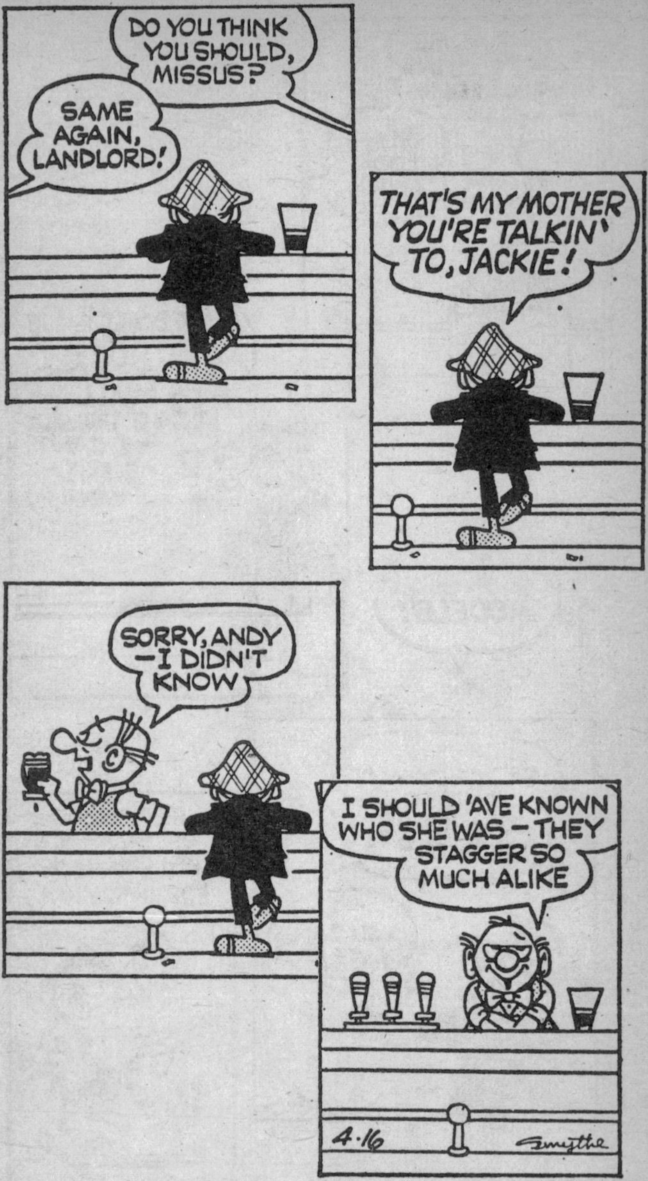
DO YOU THINK YOU SHOULD, MISSUS?
SAME AGAIN, LANDLORD!
THAT'S MY MOTHER YOU'RE TALKIN' TO, JACKIE!
SORRY, ANDY —I DIDN'T KNOW
I SHOULD 'AVE KNOWN WHO SHE WAS — THEY STAGGER SO MUCH ALIKE
4·16
Smythe

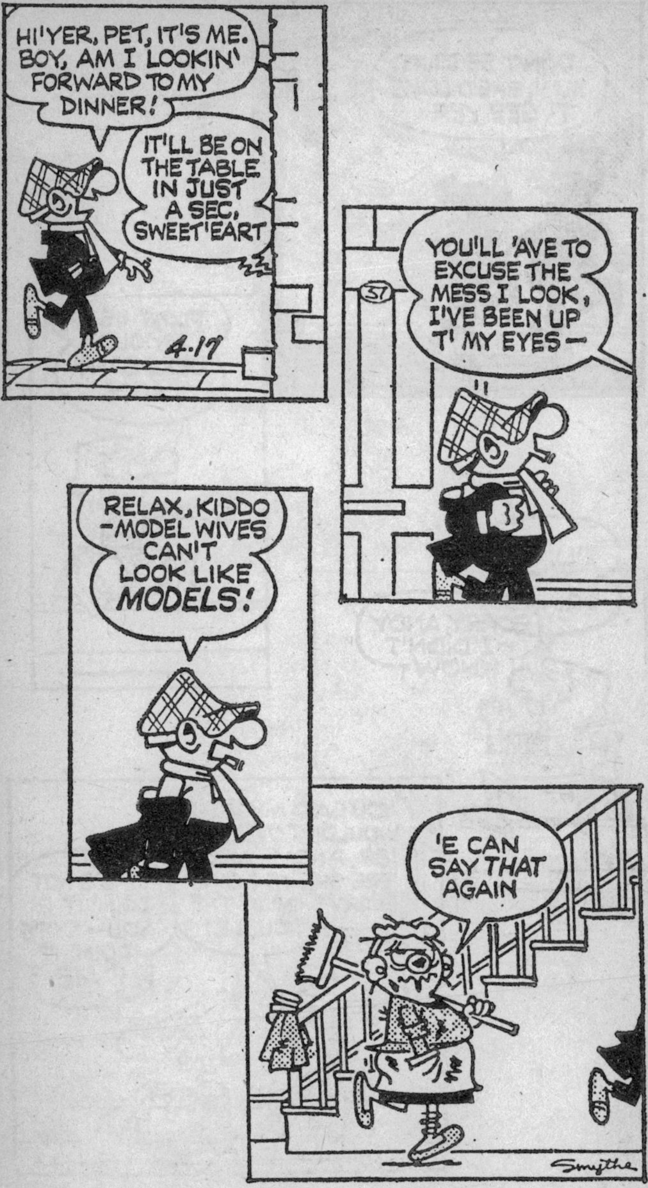
HI'YER, PET, IT'S ME. BOY, AM I LOOKIN' FORWARD TO MY DINNER!
IT'LL BE ON THE TABLE IN JUST A SEC, SWEET'EART
4.17
YOU'LL 'AVE TO EXCUSE THE MESS I LOOK, I'VE BEEN UP T' MY EYES—
RELAX, KIDDO—MODEL WIVES CAN'T LOOK LIKE *MODELS*!
'E CAN SAY *THAT* AGAIN
Smythe

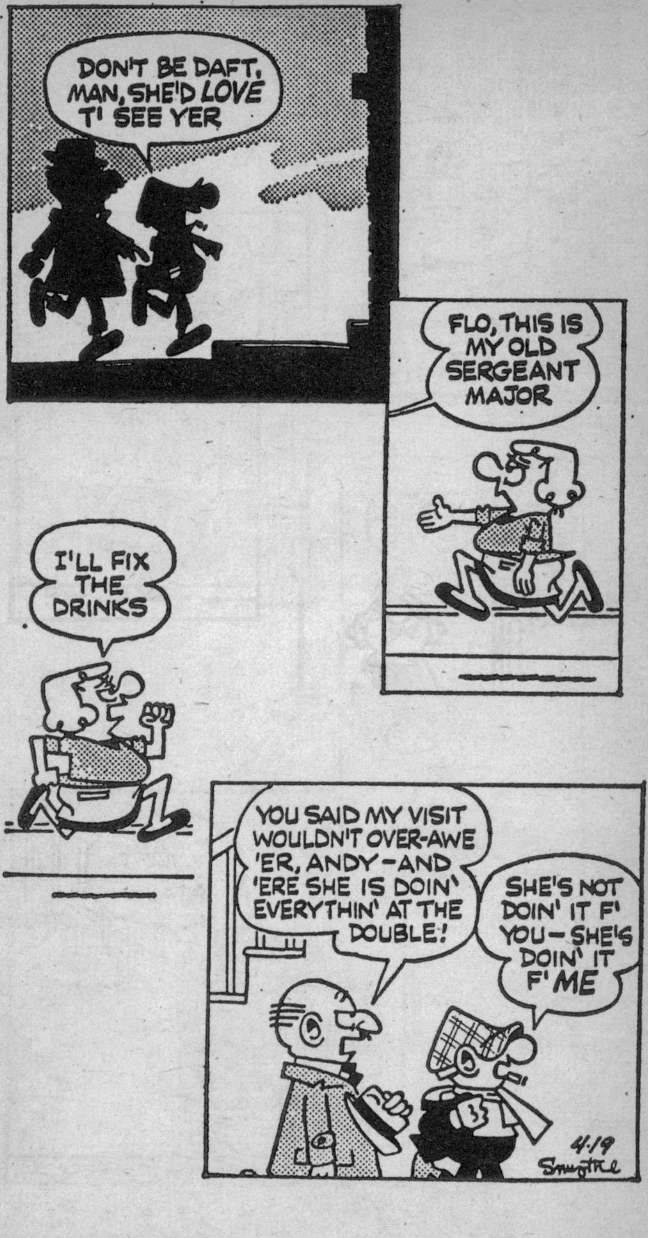
DON'T BE DAFT, MAN, SHE'D *LOVE* T' SEE YER
FLO, THIS IS MY OLD SERGEANT MAJOR
I'LL FIX THE DRINKS
YOU SAID MY VISIT WOULDN'T OVER-AWE 'ER, ANDY—AND 'ERE SHE IS DOIN' EVERYTHIN' AT THE DOUBLE!
SHE'S NOT DOIN' IT F' YOU—SHE'S DOIN' IT F' *ME*
4·19
Smythe

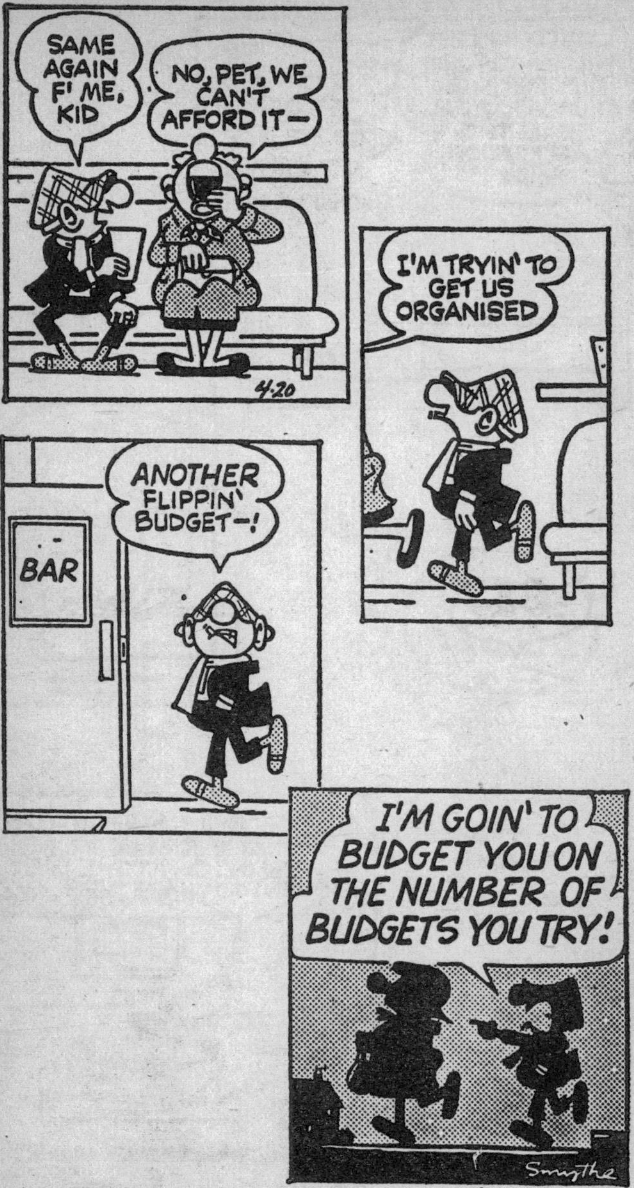
SAME AGAIN F' ME, KID
NO, PET, WE CAN'T AFFORD IT—
4·20
I'M TRYIN' TO GET US ORGANISED
ANOTHER FLIPPIN' BUDGET—!
BAR
I'M GOIN' TO BUDGET YOU ON THE NUMBER OF BUDGETS YOU TRY!
Smythe

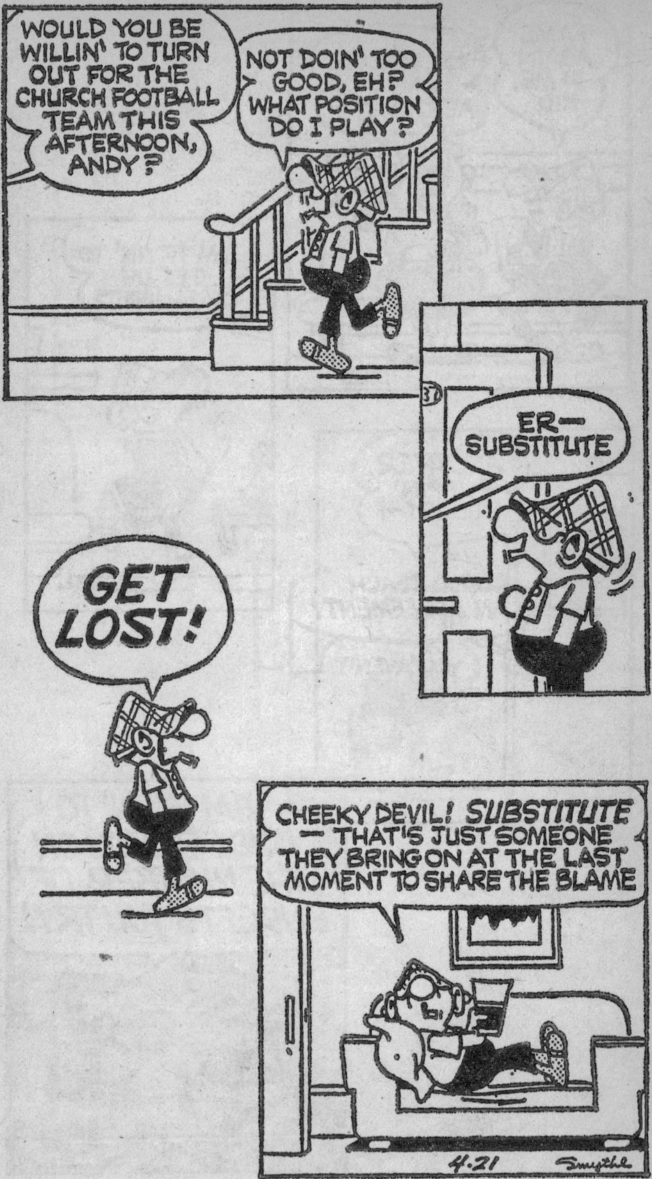
WOULD YOU BE WILLIN' TO TURN OUT FOR THE CHURCH FOOTBALL TEAM THIS AFTERNOON, ANDY?
NOT DOIN' TOO GOOD, EH? WHAT POSITION DO I PLAY?
ER— SUBSTITUTE
GET LOST!
CHEEKY DEVIL! SUBSTITUTE — THAT'S JUST SOMEONE THEY BRING ON AT THE LAST MOMENT TO SHARE THE BLAME
4.21
Smythe

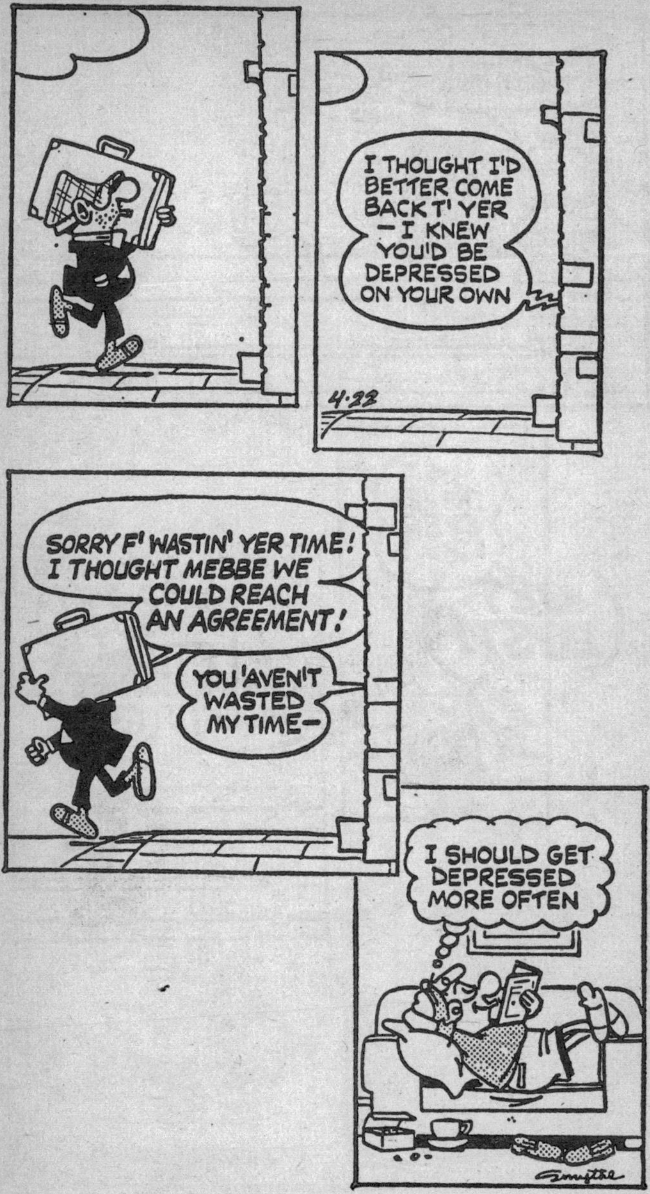
I THOUGHT I'D BETTER COME BACK T' YER —I KNEW YOU'D BE DEPRESSED ON YOUR OWN
4·22
SORRY F' WASTIN' YER TIME! I THOUGHT MEBBE WE COULD REACH AN AGREEMENT!
YOU 'AVEN'T WASTED MY TIME—
I SHOULD GET DEPRESSED MORE OFTEN
Smythe

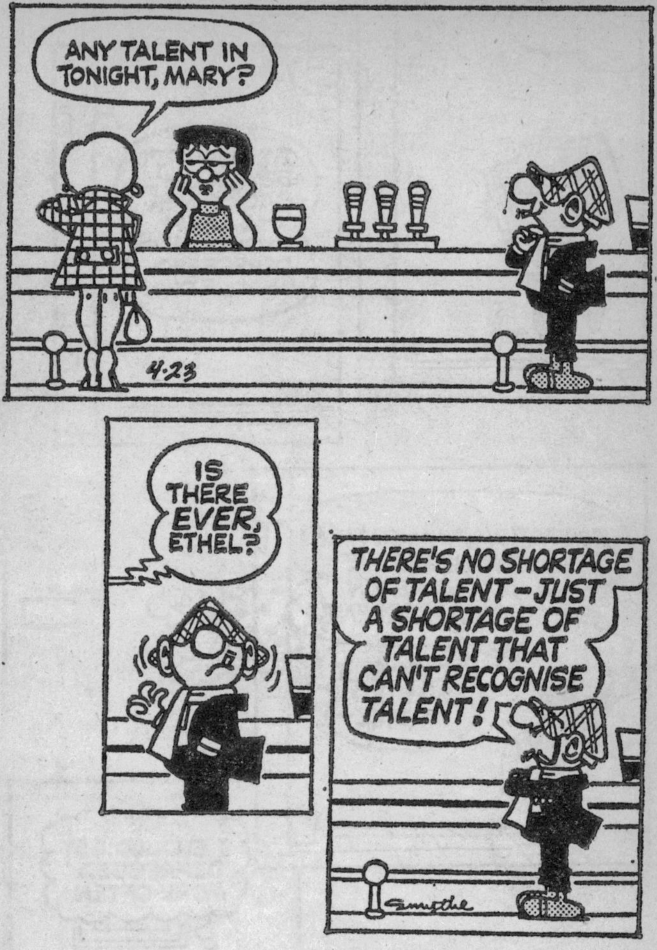
ANY TALENT IN TONIGHT, MARY?
4·23
IS THERE EVER, ETHEL?
THERE'S NO SHORTAGE OF TALENT – JUST A SHORTAGE OF TALENT THAT CAN'T RECOGNISE TALENT!
Smythe

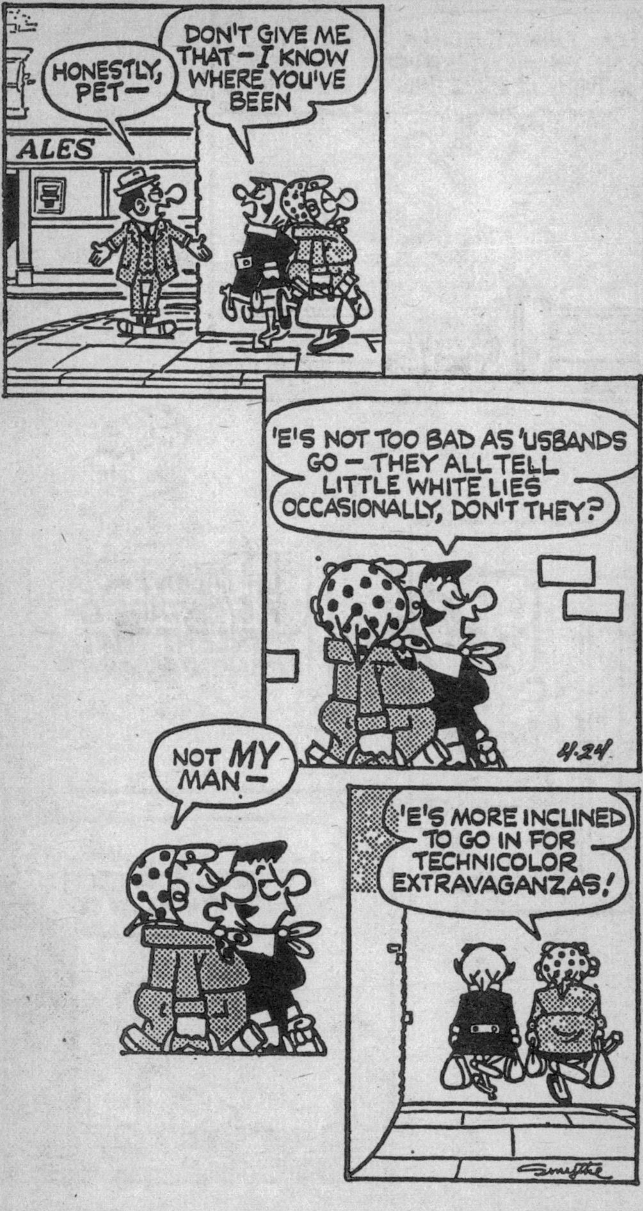
ALES
HONESTLY, PET—
DON'T GIVE ME THAT—I KNOW WHERE YOU'VE BEEN
'E'S NOT TOO BAD AS 'USBANDS GO—THEY ALL TELL LITTLE WHITE LIES OCCASIONALLY, DON'T THEY?
4·24
NOT MY MAN—
'E'S MORE INCLINED TO GO IN FOR TECHNICOLOR EXTRAVAGANZAS!
Smythe

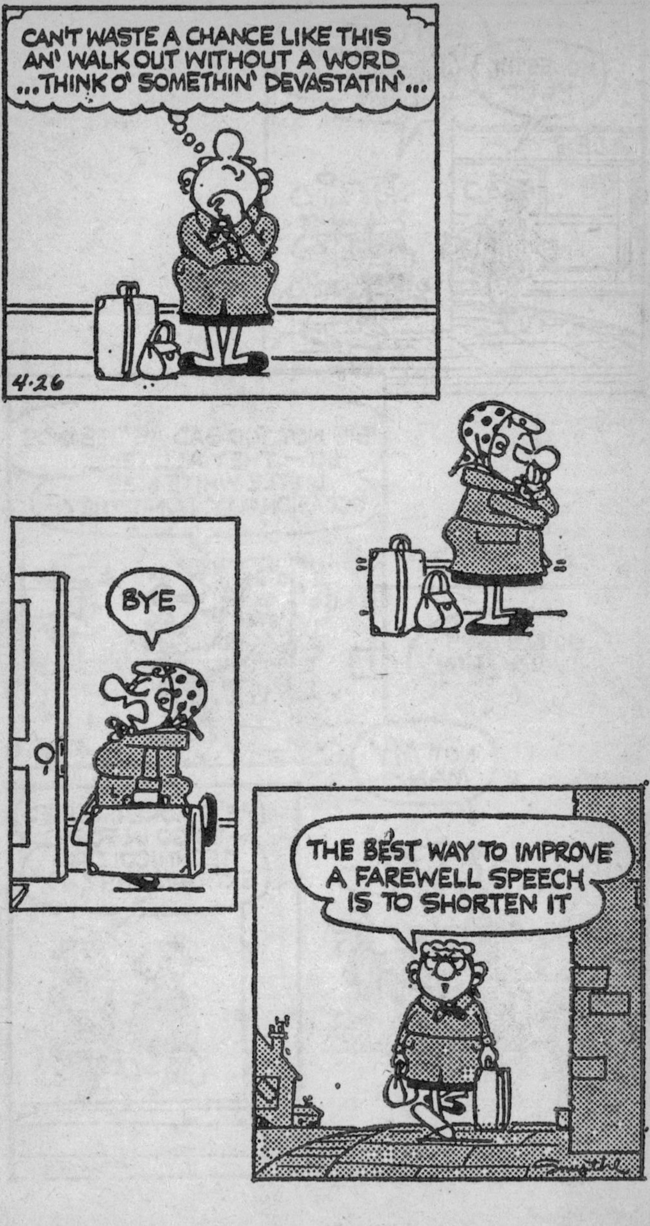
CAN'T WASTE A CHANCE LIKE THIS AN' WALK OUT WITHOUT A WORD ...THINK O' SOMETHIN' DEVASTATIN'...
4·26
BYE
THE BEST WAY TO IMPROVE A FAREWELL SPEECH IS TO SHORTEN IT

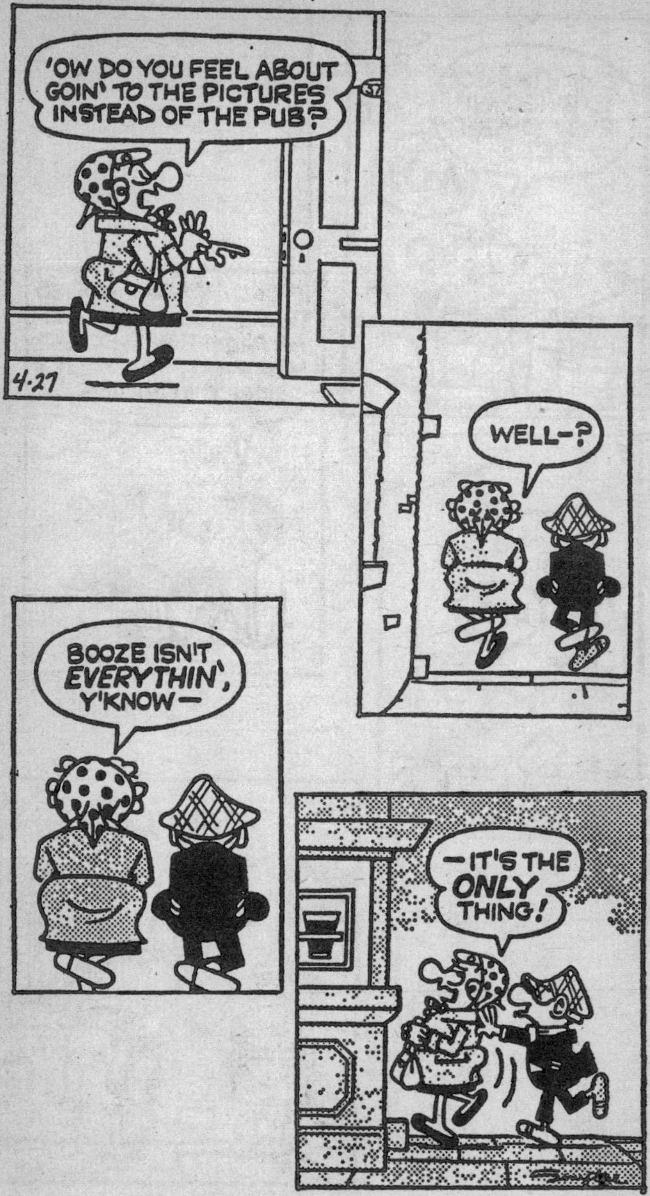
'OW DO YOU FEEL ABOUT GOIN' TO THE PICTURES INSTEAD OF THE PUB?
4-27
WELL-?
BOOZE ISN'T *EVERYTHIN'*, Y'KNOW—
—IT'S THE *ONLY* THING!

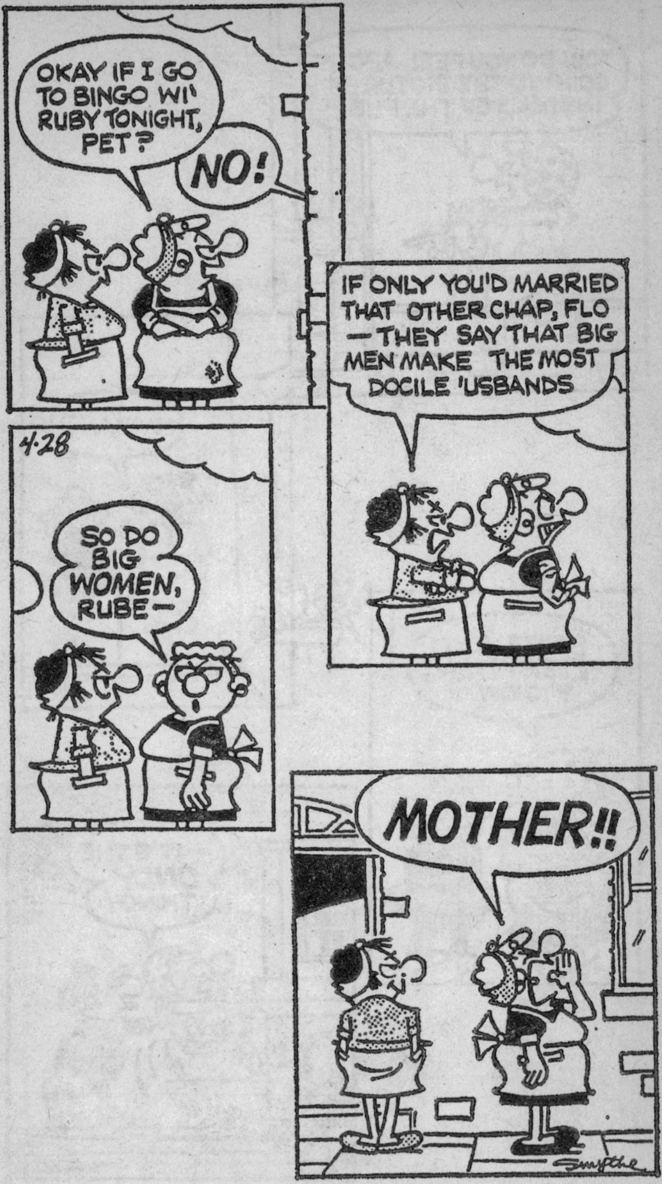
OKAY IF I GO TO BINGO WI' RUBY TONIGHT, PET?
NO!
IF ONLY YOU'D MARRIED THAT OTHER CHAP, FLO — THEY SAY THAT BIG MEN MAKE THE MOST DOCILE 'USBANDS
4·28
SO DO BIG WOMEN, RUBE—
MOTHER!!
Smythe

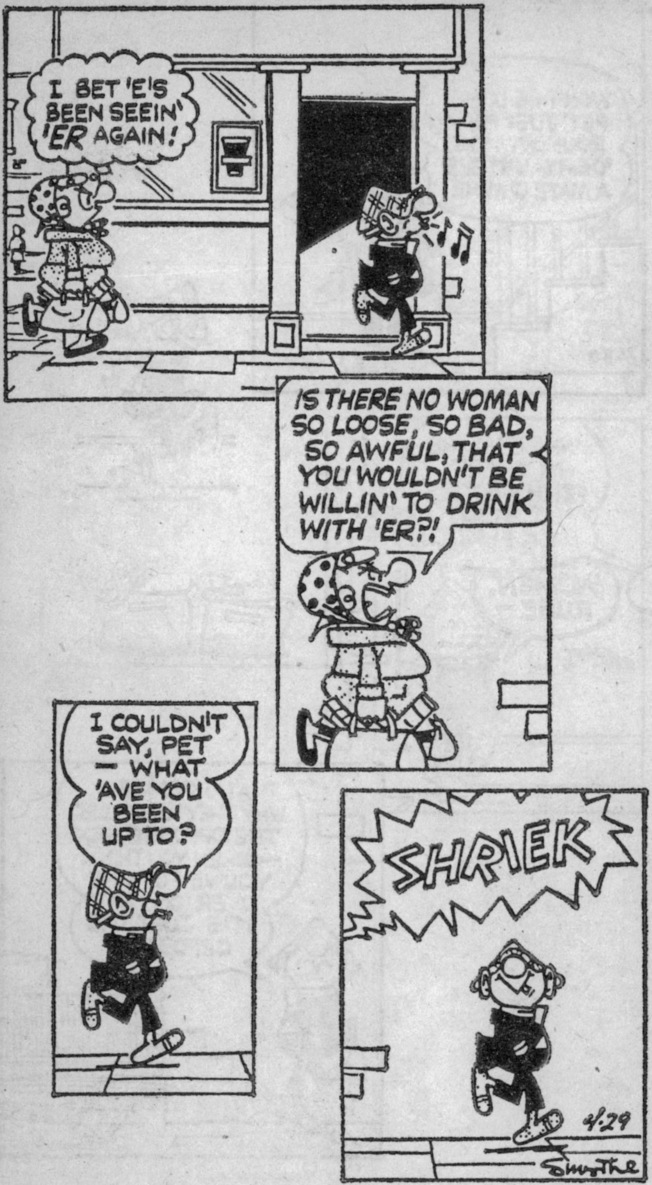
I BET 'E'S BEEN SEEIN' 'ER AGAIN!
IS THERE NO WOMAN SO LOOSE, SO BAD, SO AWFUL, THAT YOU WOULDN'T BE WILLIN' TO DRINK WITH 'ER?!
I COULDN'T SAY, PET — WHAT 'AVE YOU BEEN UP TO?
SHRIEK
4·29
Smythe

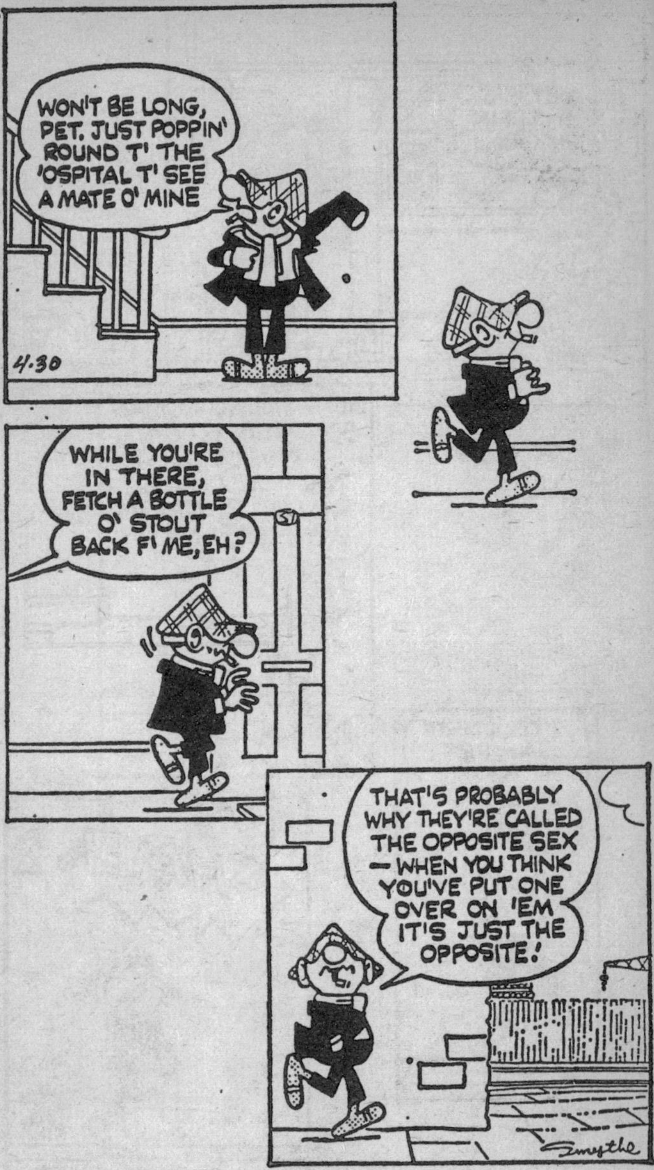
WON'T BE LONG, PET. JUST POPPIN' ROUND T' THE 'OSPITAL T' SEE A MATE O' MINE
4.30
WHILE YOU'RE IN THERE, FETCH A BOTTLE O' STOUT BACK F' ME, EH?
THAT'S PROBABLY WHY THEY'RE CALLED THE OPPOSITE SEX — WHEN YOU THINK YOU'VE PUT ONE OVER ON 'EM IT'S JUST THE OPPOSITE!
Smythe

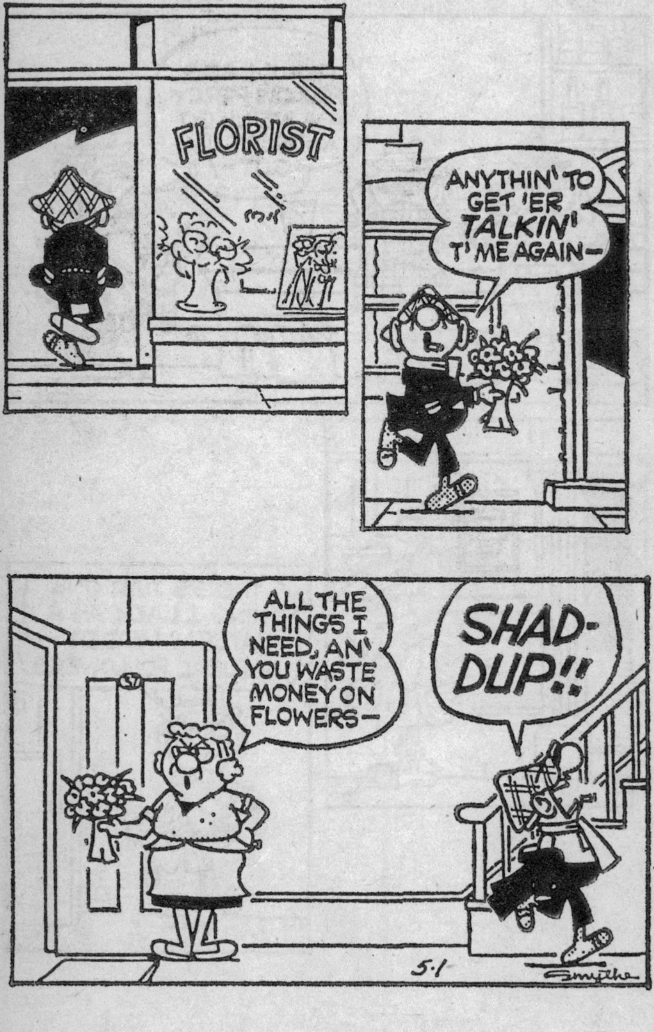
FLORIST
ANYTHIN' TO GET 'ER TALKIN' T' ME AGAIN—
ALL THE THINGS I NEED, AN' YOU WASTE MONEY ON FLOWERS—
SHAD-DUP!!
5·1
Smythe

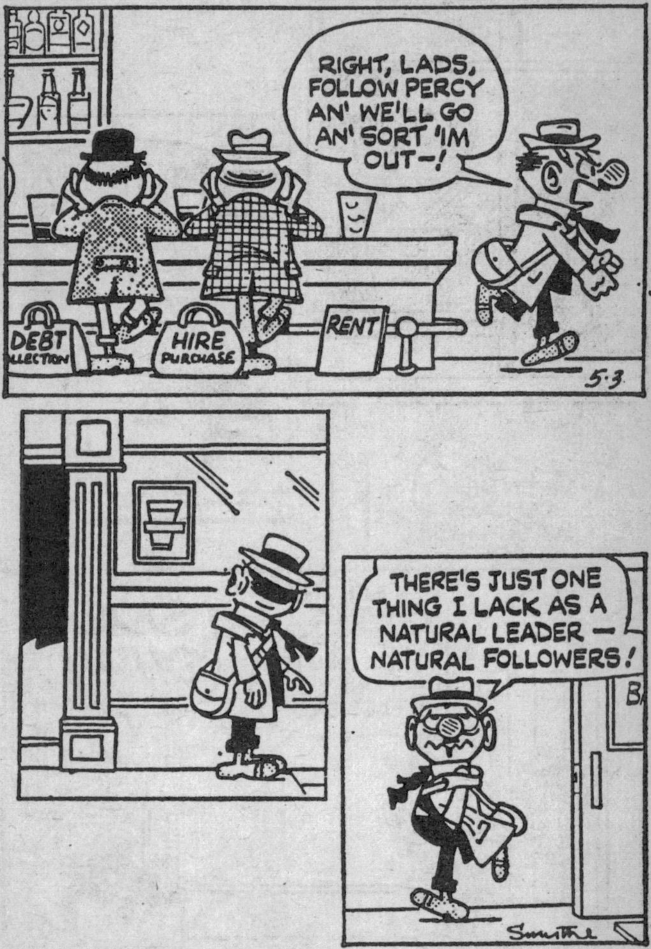
RIGHT, LADS, FOLLOW PERCY AN' WE'LL GO AN' SORT 'IM OUT–!
DEBT
HIRE PURCHASE
RENT
5·3
THERE'S JUST ONE THING I LACK AS A NATURAL LEADER — NATURAL FOLLOWERS!
Smythe

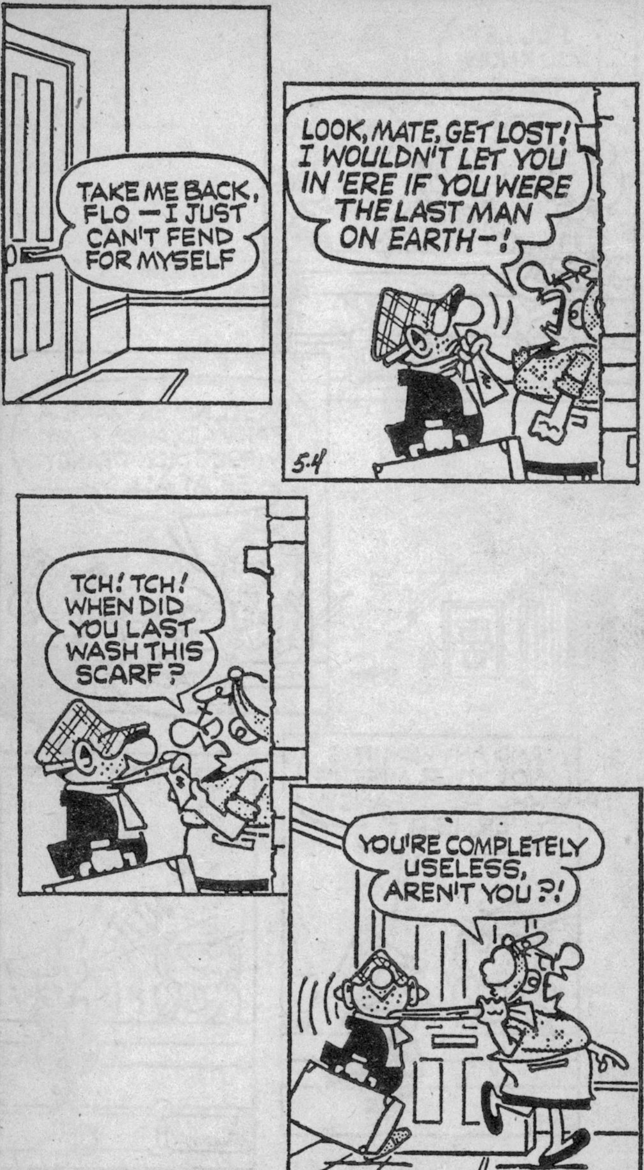
TAKE ME BACK, FLO — I JUST CAN'T FEND FOR MYSELF
LOOK, MATE, GET LOST! I WOULDN'T LET YOU IN 'ERE IF YOU WERE THE LAST MAN ON EARTH—!
5-4
TCH! TCH! WHEN DID YOU LAST WASH THIS SCARF?
YOU'RE COMPLETELY USELESS, AREN'T YOU ?!

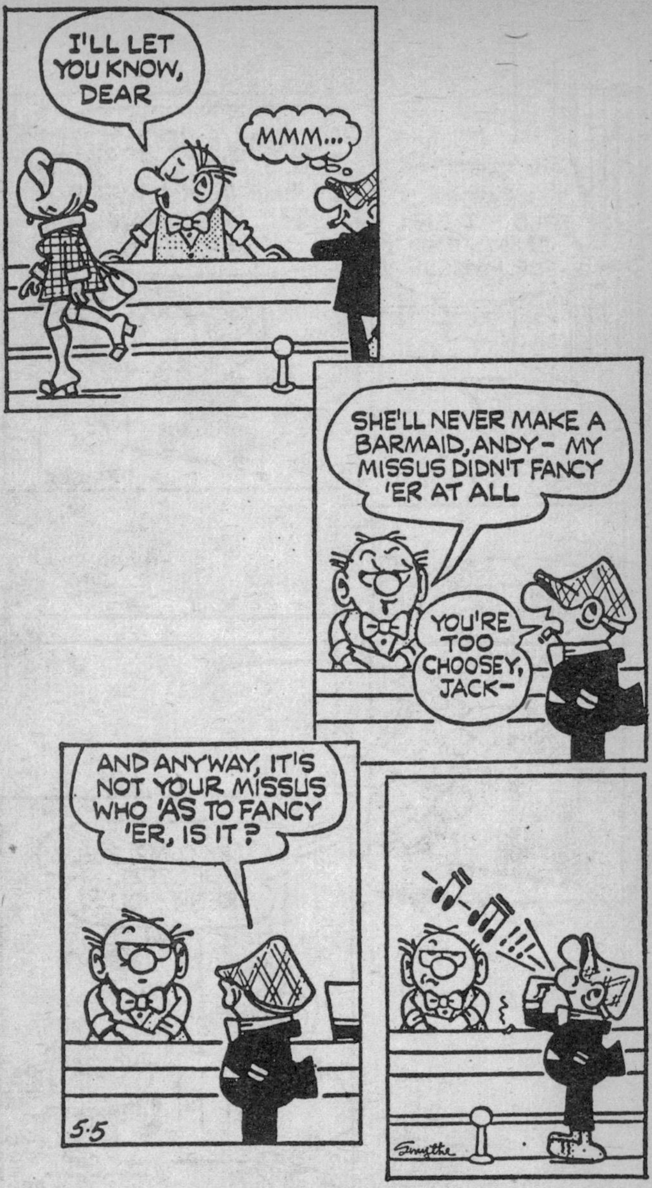
I'LL LET YOU KNOW, DEAR
MMM...
SHE'LL NEVER MAKE A BARMAID, ANDY - MY MISSUS DIDN'T FANCY 'ER AT ALL
YOU'RE TOO CHOOSEY, JACK-
AND ANYWAY, IT'S NOT YOUR MISSUS WHO 'AS TO FANCY 'ER, IS IT?
5·5
Smythe

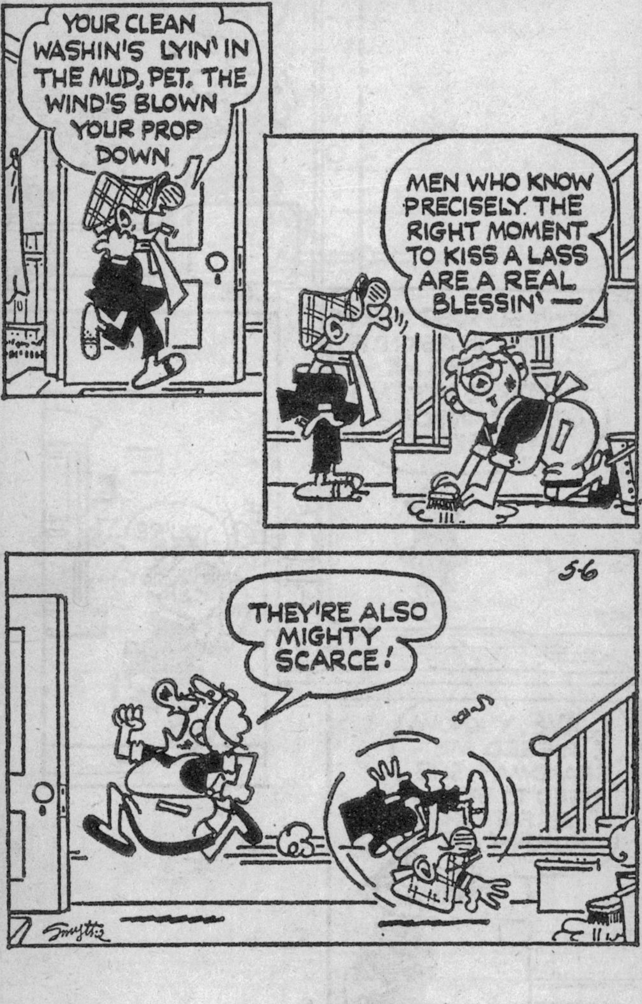
YOUR CLEAN WASHIN'S LYIN' IN THE MUD, PET. THE WIND'S BLOWN YOUR PROP DOWN
MEN WHO KNOW PRECISELY THE RIGHT MOMENT TO KISS A LASS ARE A REAL BLESSIN' —
5-6
THEY'RE ALSO MIGHTY SCARCE!
Smythe

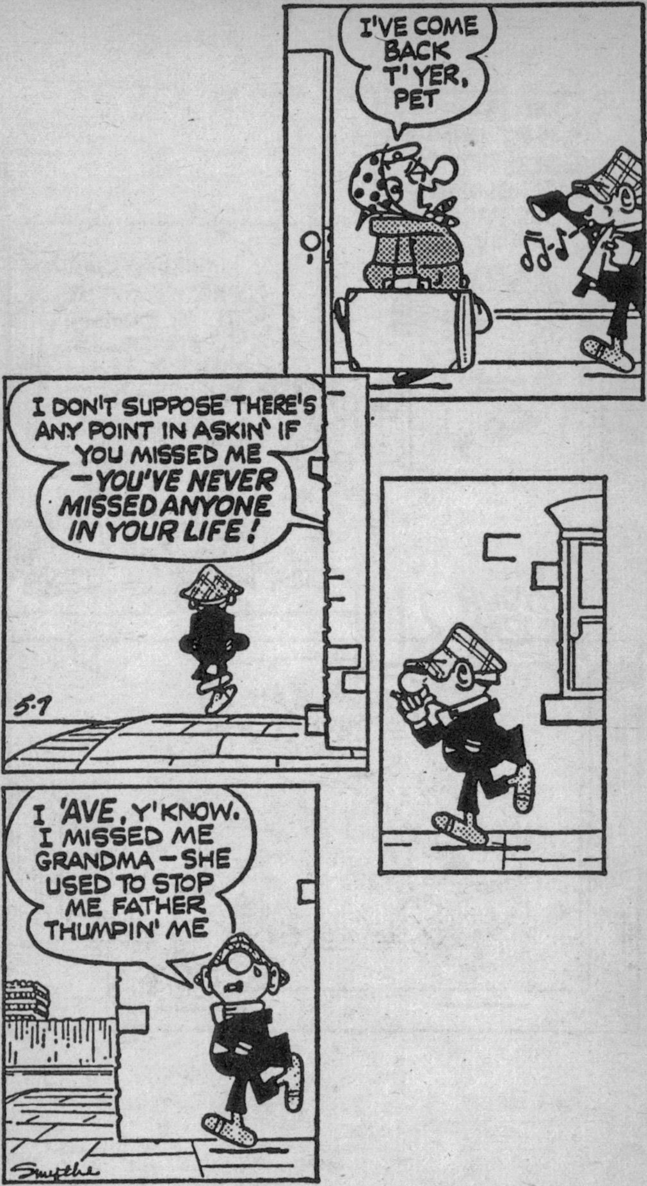
I'VE COME BACK T'YER, PET
I DON'T SUPPOSE THERE'S ANY POINT IN ASKIN' IF YOU MISSED ME —*YOU'VE NEVER MISSED ANYONE IN YOUR LIFE!*
5·7
I 'AVE, Y'KNOW. I MISSED ME GRANDMA — SHE USED TO STOP ME FATHER THUMPIN' ME
Smythe

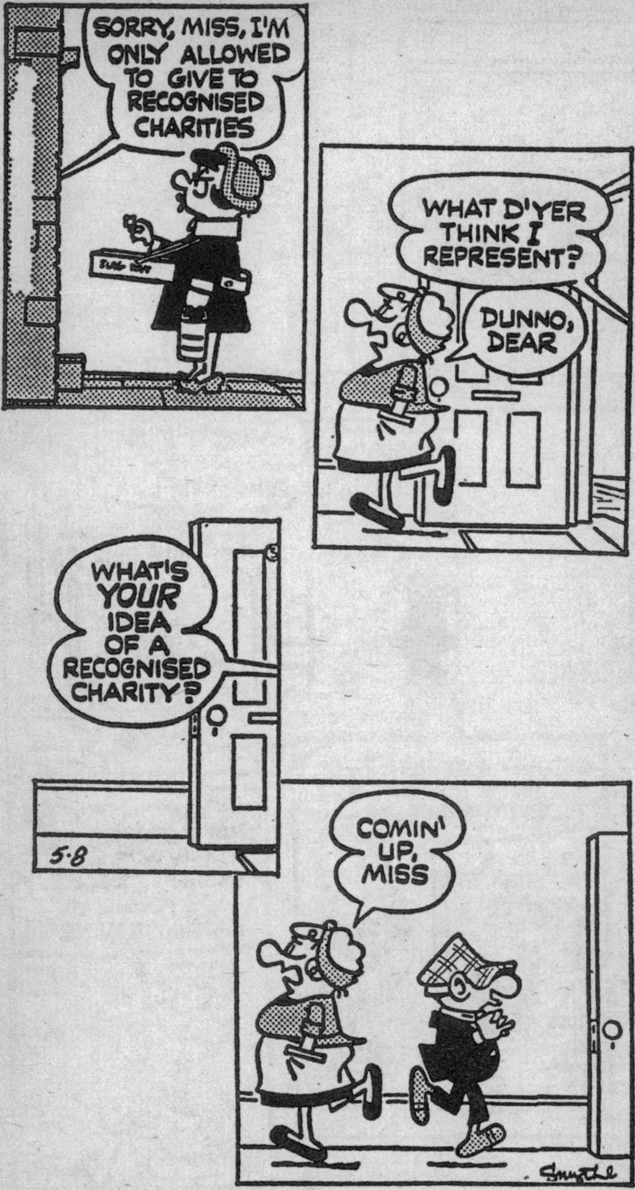
SORRY, MISS, I'M ONLY ALLOWED TO GIVE TO RECOGNISED CHARITIES
WHAT D'YER THINK I REPRESENT?
DUNNO, DEAR
WHAT'S YOUR IDEA OF A RECOGNISED CHARITY?
5·8
COMIN' UP, MISS
Smythe

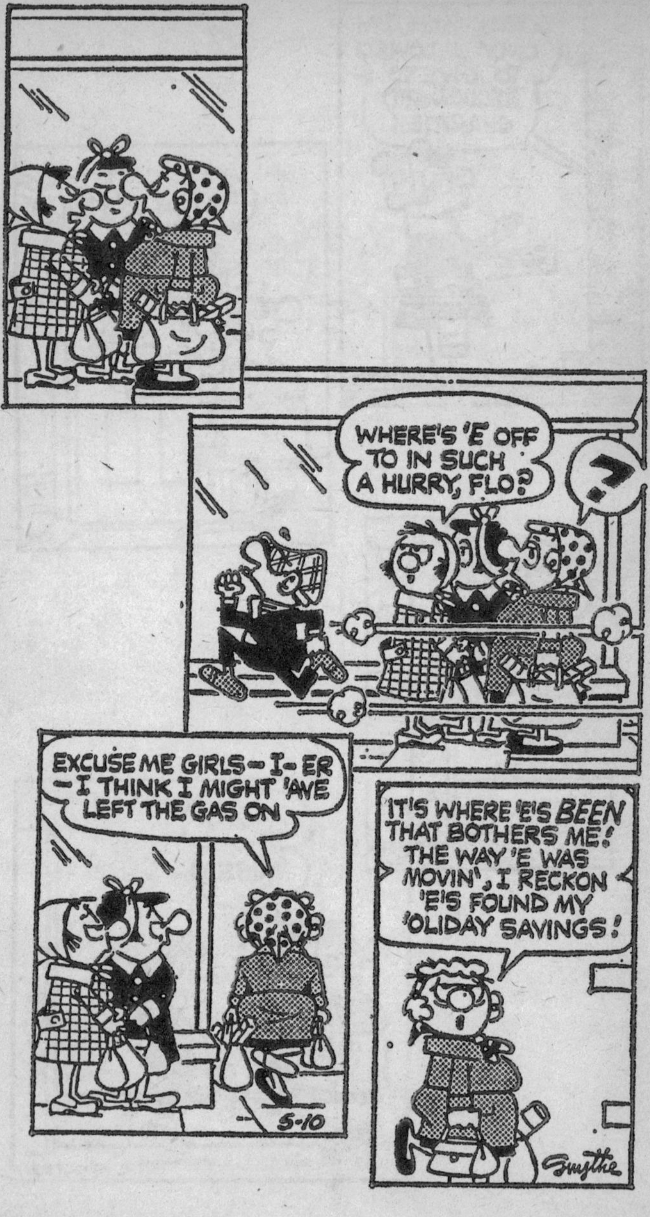
WHERE'S 'E OFF TO IN SUCH A HURRY, FLO?
?
EXCUSE ME GIRLS — I — ER — I THINK I MIGHT 'AVE LEFT THE GAS ON
IT'S WHERE 'E'S *BEEN* THAT BOTHERS ME! THE WAY 'E WAS MOVIN', I RECKON 'E'S FOUND MY 'OLIDAY SAVINGS!
5-10
Smythe

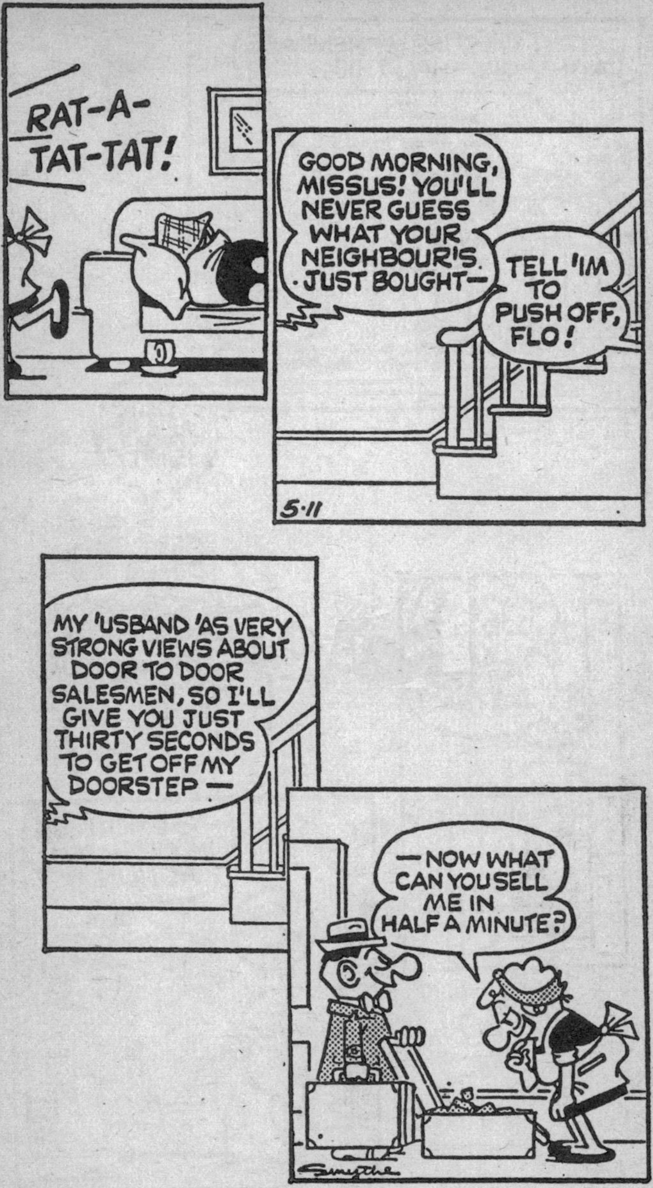
RAT-A-TAT-TAT!
GOOD MORNING, MISSUS! YOU'LL NEVER GUESS WHAT YOUR NEIGHBOUR'S JUST BOUGHT—
TELL 'IM TO PUSH OFF, FLO!
5·11
MY 'USBAND 'AS VERY STRONG VIEWS ABOUT DOOR TO DOOR SALESMEN, SO I'LL GIVE YOU JUST THIRTY SECONDS TO GET OFF MY DOORSTEP —
— NOW WHAT CAN YOU SELL ME IN HALF A MINUTE?
Smythe

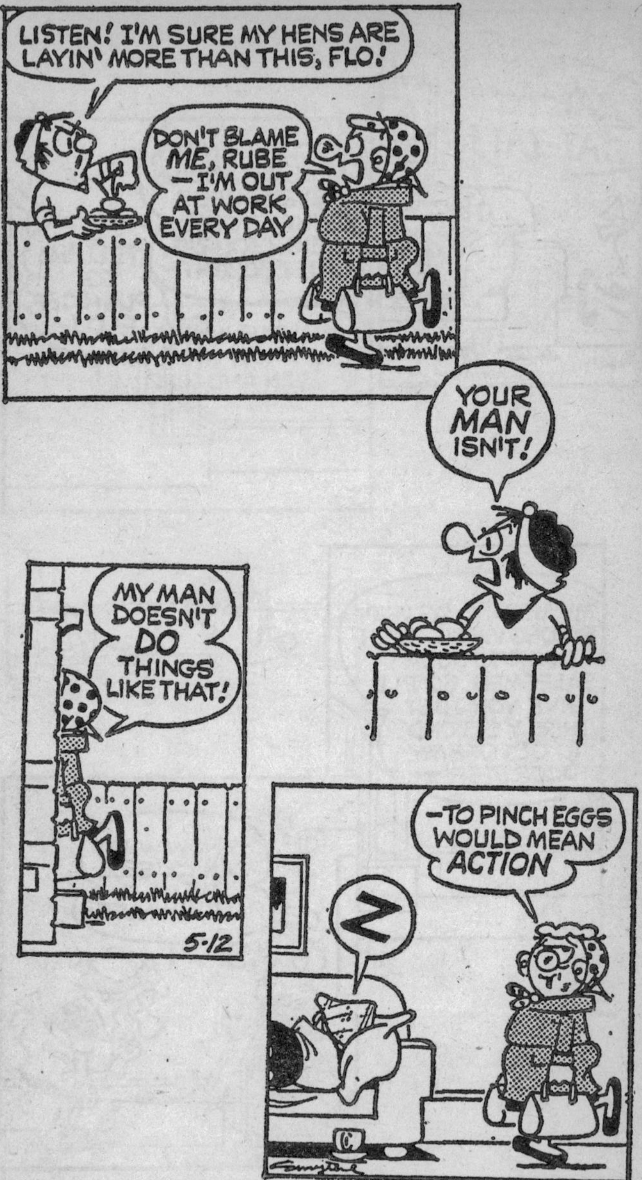

LISTEN! I'M SURE MY HENS ARE LAYIN' MORE THAN THIS, FLO!
DON'T BLAME ME, RUBE —I'M OUT AT WORK EVERY DAY
YOUR MAN ISN'T!
MY MAN DOESN'T DO THINGS LIKE THAT!
5-12
—TO PINCH EGGS WOULD MEAN ACTION
Z

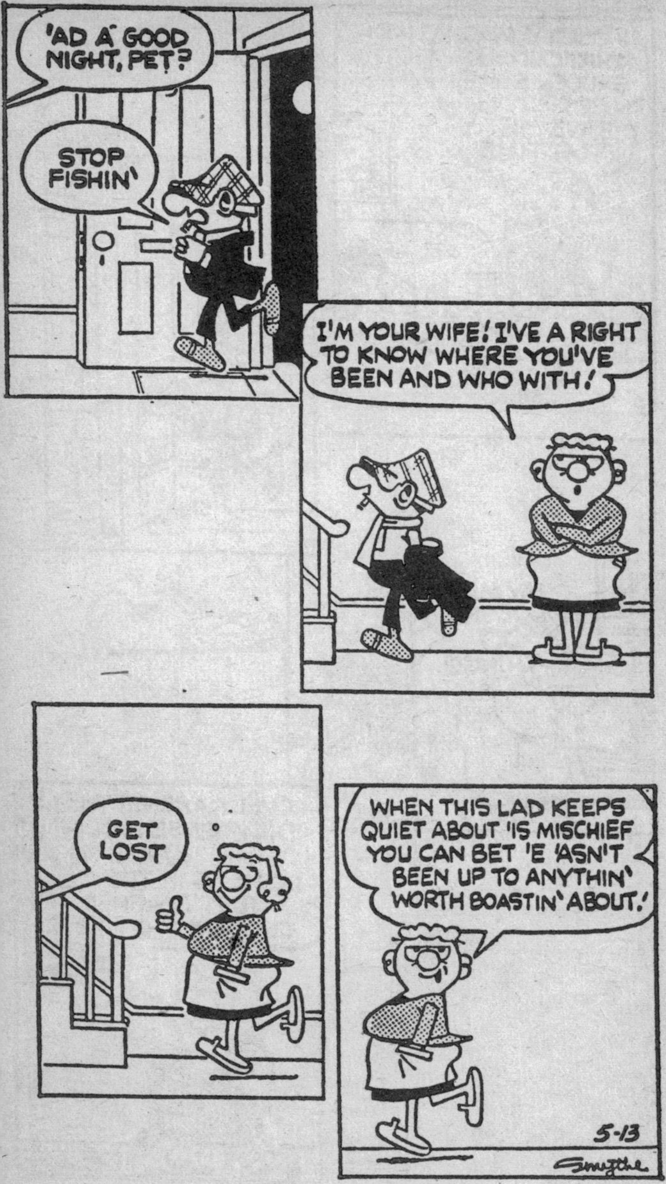
'AD A GOOD NIGHT, PET?
STOP FISHIN'
I'M YOUR WIFE! I'VE A RIGHT TO KNOW WHERE YOU'VE BEEN AND WHO WITH!
GET LOST
WHEN THIS LAD KEEPS QUIET ABOUT 'IS MISCHIEF YOU CAN BET 'E 'ASN'T BEEN UP TO ANYTHIN' WORTH BOASTIN' ABOUT.'
5-13
Smythe

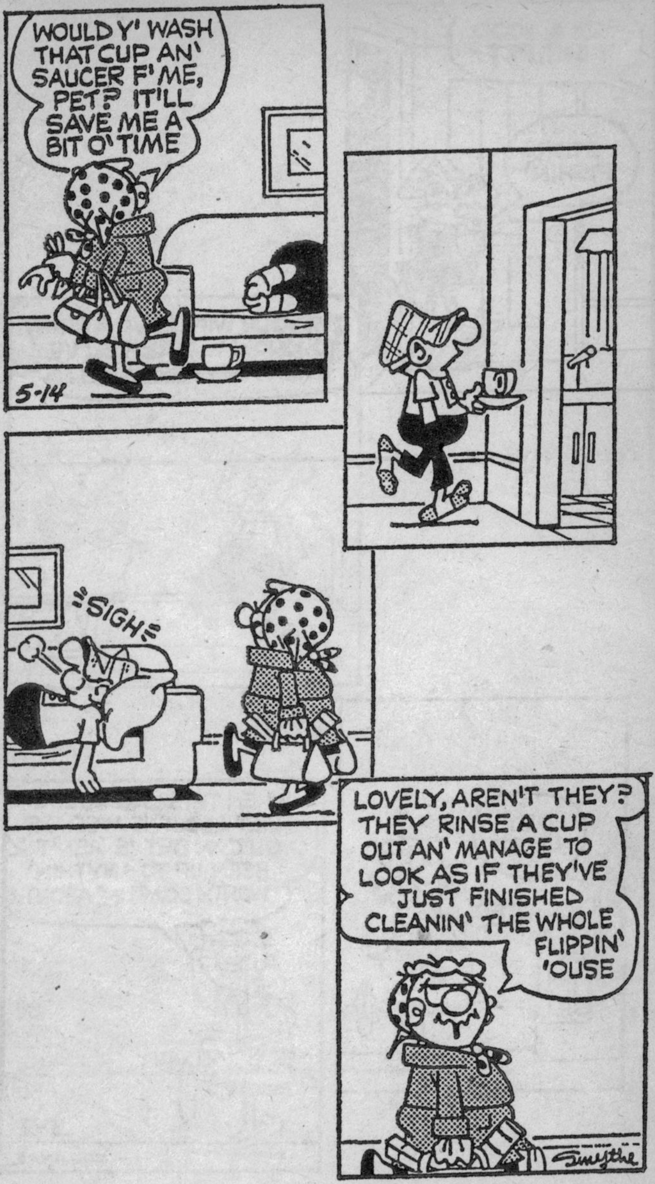
WOULD Y' WASH THAT CUP AN' SAUCER F' ME, PET? IT'LL SAVE ME A BIT O' TIME
5-14
SIGH
LOVELY, AREN'T THEY? THEY RINSE A CUP OUT AN' MANAGE TO LOOK AS IF THEY'VE JUST FINISHED CLEANIN' THE WHOLE FLIPPIN' 'OUSE
Smythe

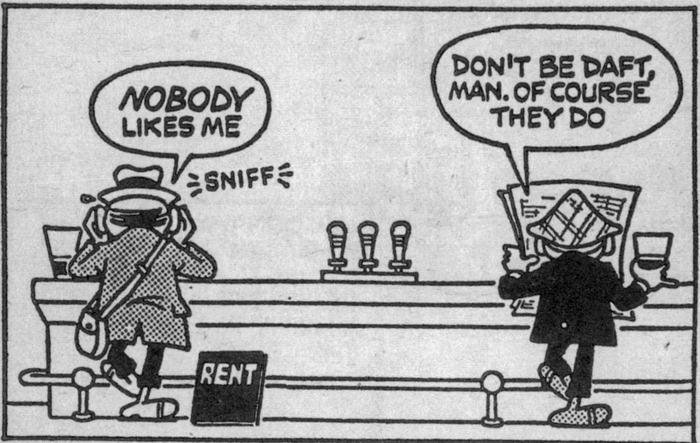
NOBODY LIKES ME
SNIFF
DON'T BE DAFT, MAN. OF COURSE THEY DO
RENT

5-15

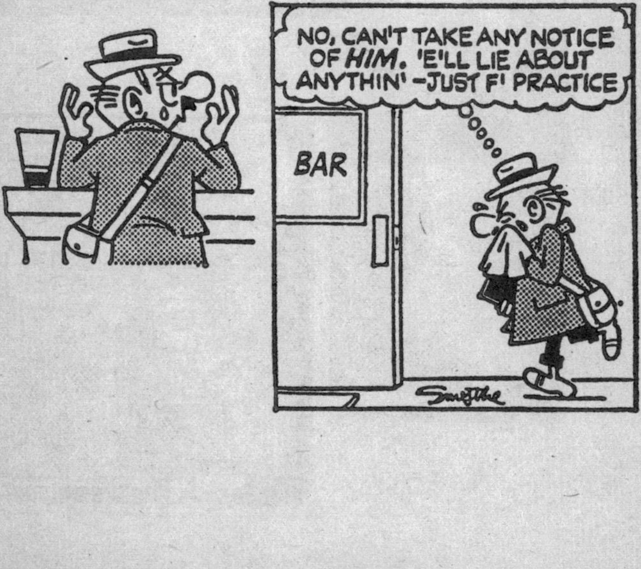
NO, CAN'T TAKE ANY NOTICE OF *HIM*. 'E'LL LIE ABOUT ANYTHIN' –JUST F' PRACTICE
BAR
Smythe

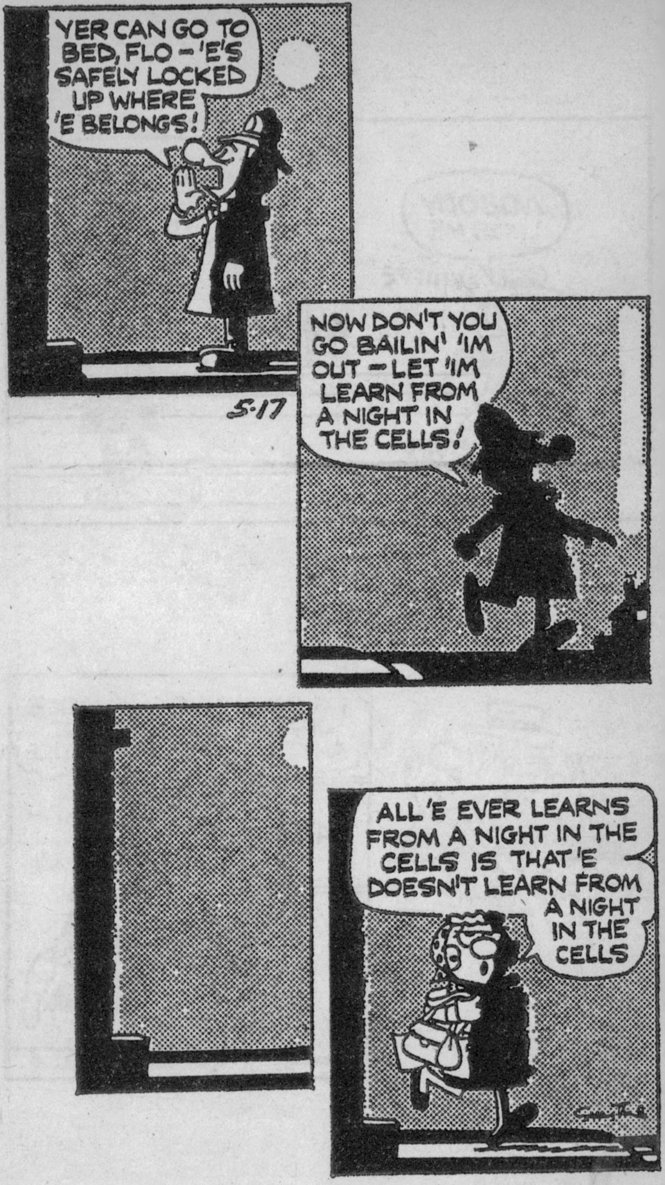
YER CAN GO TO BED, FLO – 'E'S SAFELY LOCKED UP WHERE 'E BELONGS!
5·17
NOW DON'T YOU GO BAILIN' 'IM OUT – LET 'IM LEARN FROM A NIGHT IN THE CELLS!
ALL 'E EVER LEARNS FROM A NIGHT IN THE CELLS IS THAT 'E DOESN'T LEARN FROM A NIGHT IN THE CELLS

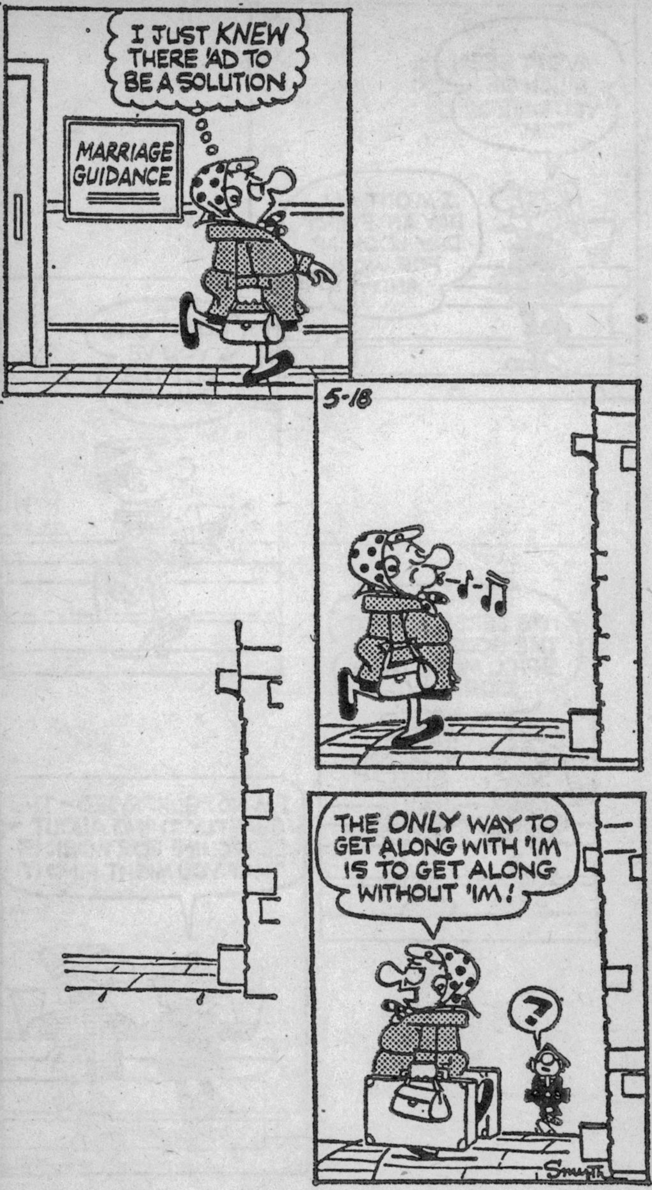
I JUST KNEW THERE 'AD TO BE A SOLUTION!
MARRIAGE GUIDANCE
5-18
THE ONLY WAY TO GET ALONG WITH 'IM IS TO GET ALONG WITHOUT 'IM!
?
Smyth

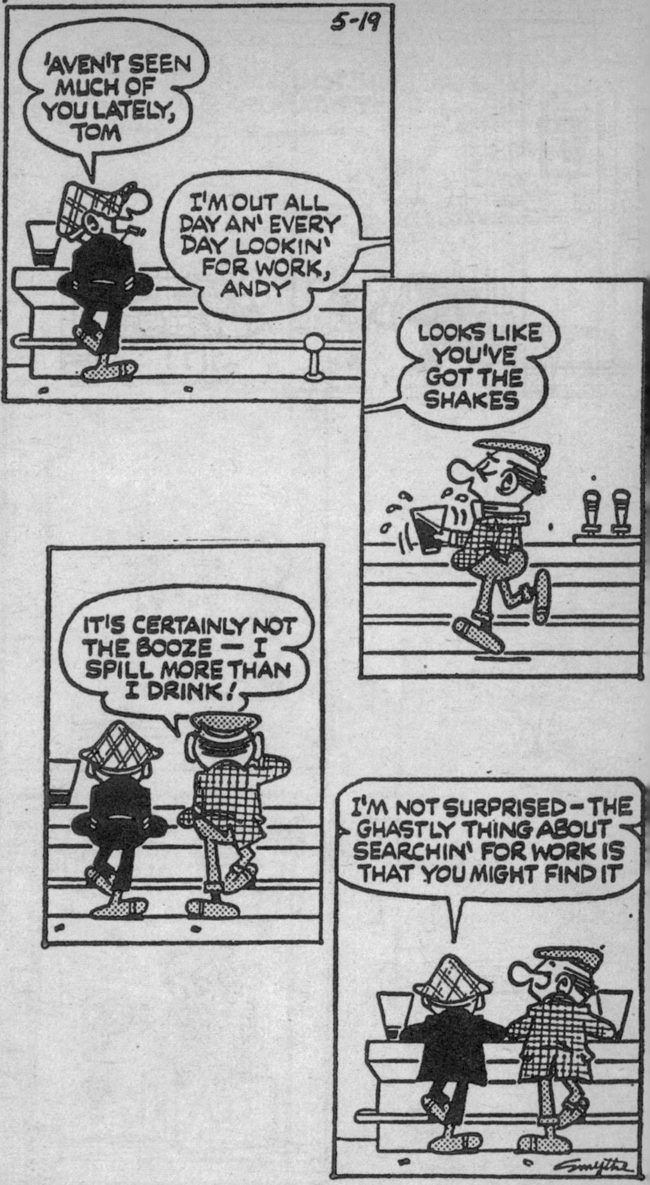
5-19
'AVEN'T SEEN MUCH OF YOU LATELY, TOM
I'M OUT ALL DAY AN' EVERY DAY LOOKIN' FOR WORK, ANDY
LOOKS LIKE YOU'VE GOT THE SHAKES
IT'S CERTAINLY NOT THE BOOZE — I SPILL MORE THAN I DRINK!
I'M NOT SURPRISED — THE GHASTLY THING ABOUT SEARCHIN' FOR WORK IS THAT YOU MIGHT FIND IT
Smythe

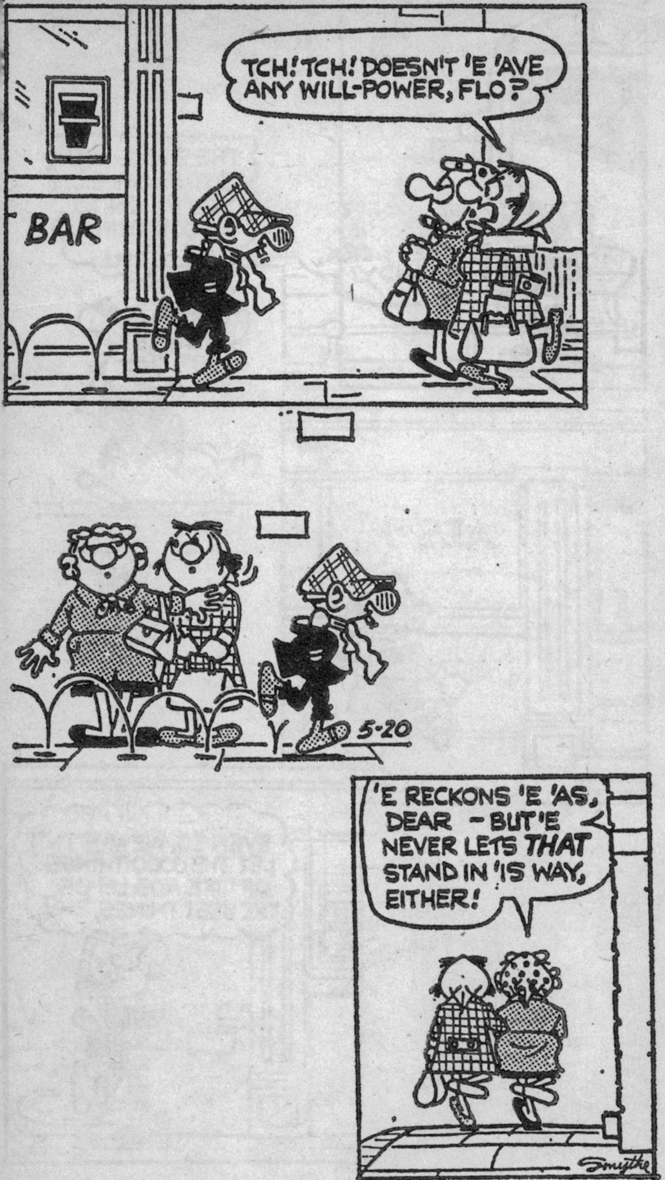
BAR
TCH! TCH! DOESN'T 'E 'AVE ANY WILL-POWER, FLO?
5-20
'E RECKONS 'E 'AS, DEAR - BUT 'E NEVER LETS *THAT* STAND IN 'IS WAY, EITHER!
Smythe

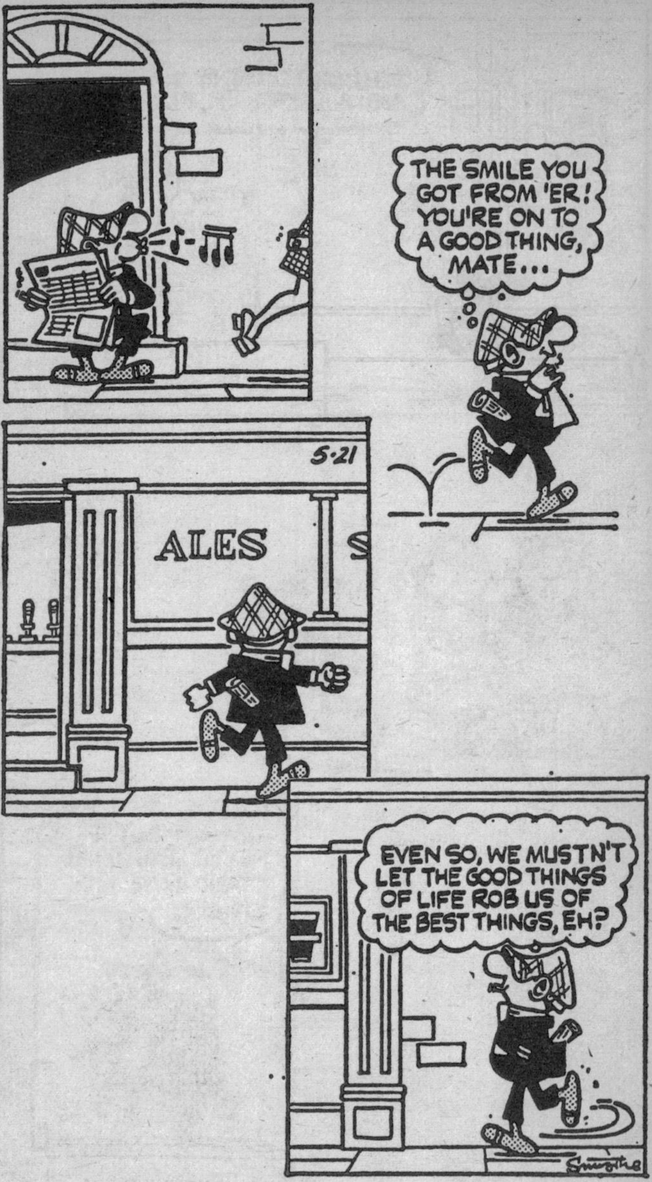
THE SMILE YOU GOT FROM 'ER! YOU'RE ON TO A GOOD THING, MATE...
5·21
ALES
EVEN SO, WE MUSTN'T LET THE GOOD THINGS OF LIFE ROB US OF THE BEST THINGS, EH?
Smythe

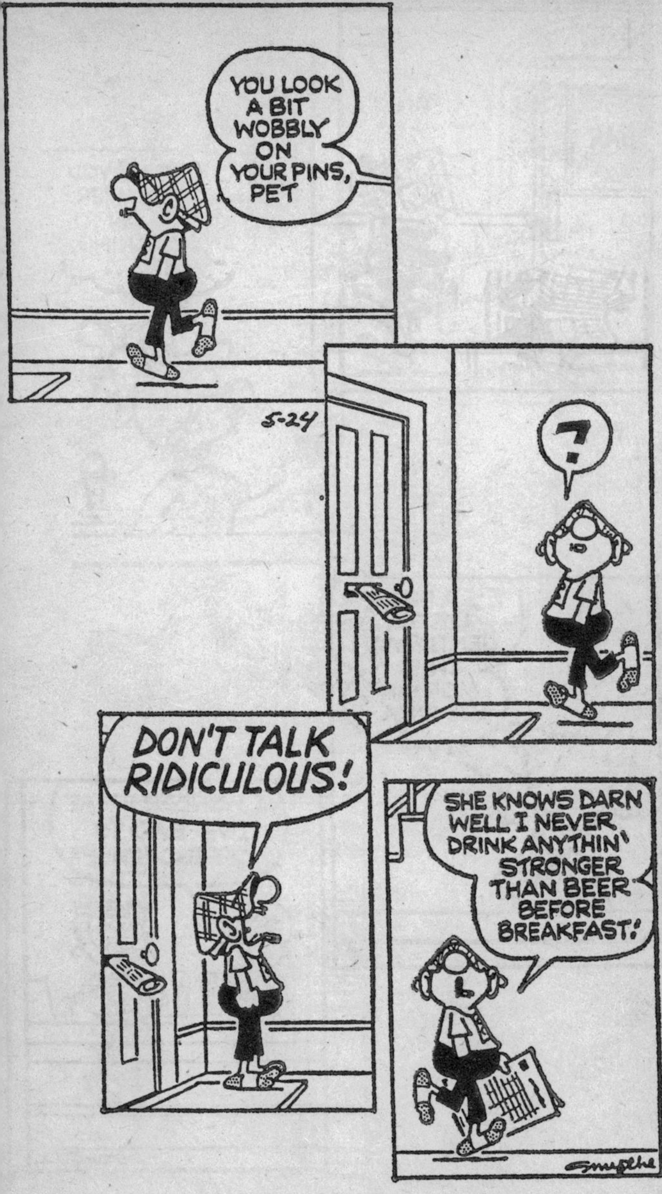
YOU LOOK A BIT WOBBLY ON YOUR PINS, PET
5-24
?
DON'T TALK RIDICULOUS!
SHE KNOWS DARN WELL I NEVER DRINK ANYTHIN' STRONGER THAN BEER BEFORE BREAKFAST!
Smythe

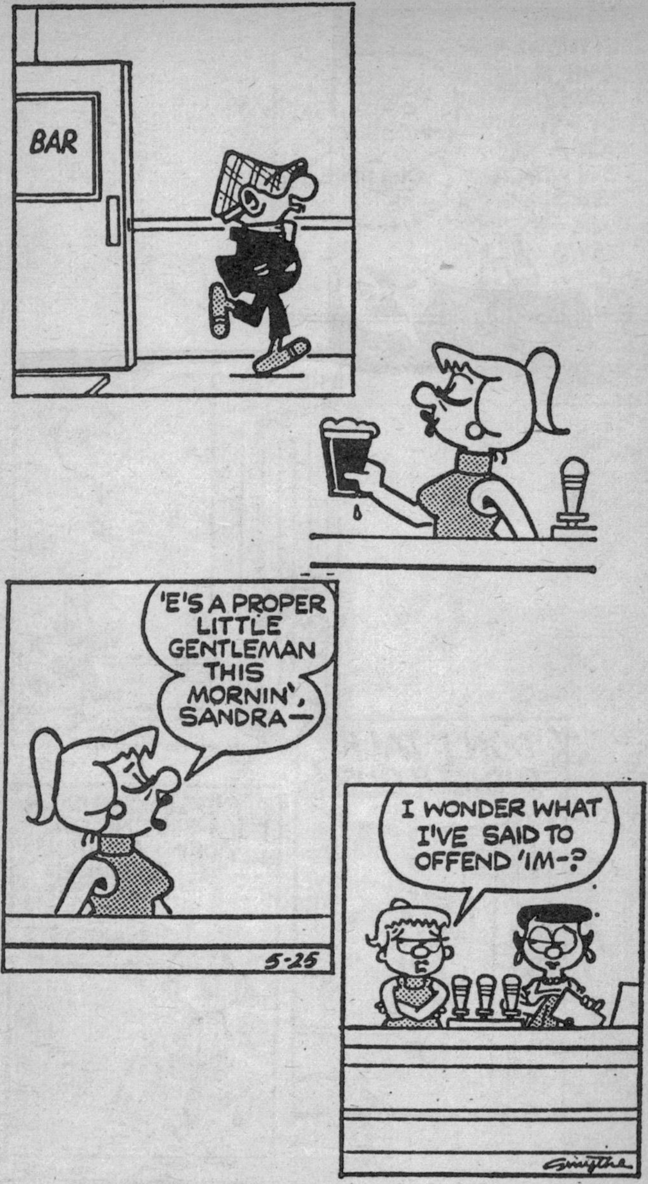
BAR
'E'S A PROPER LITTLE GENTLEMAN THIS MORNIN', SANDRA—
5-25
I WONDER WHAT I'VE SAID TO OFFEND 'IM-?
Smythe

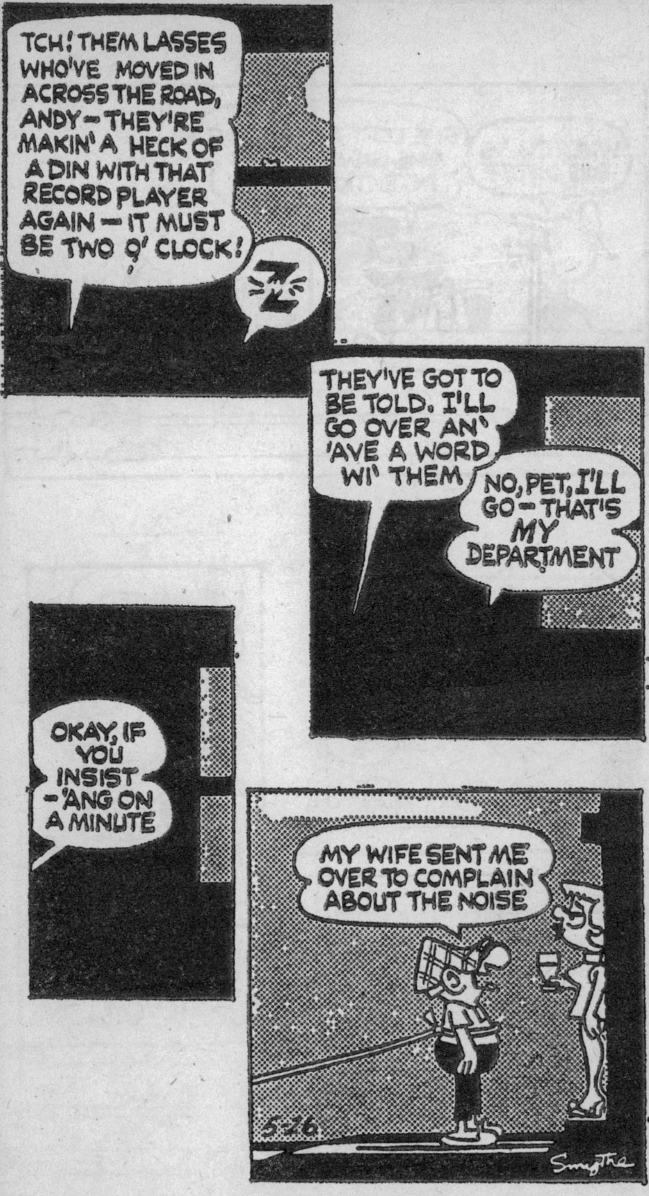
TCH! THEM LASSES WHO'VE MOVED IN ACROSS THE ROAD, ANDY – THEY'RE MAKIN' A HECK OF A DIN WITH THAT RECORD PLAYER AGAIN – IT MUST BE TWO O' CLOCK!
THEY'VE GOT TO BE TOLD. I'LL GO OVER AN' 'AVE A WORD WI' THEM
NO, PET, I'LL GO – THAT'S MY DEPARTMENT
OKAY, IF YOU INSIST – 'ANG ON A MINUTE
MY WIFE SENT ME OVER TO COMPLAIN ABOUT THE NOISE
5-26
Smythe

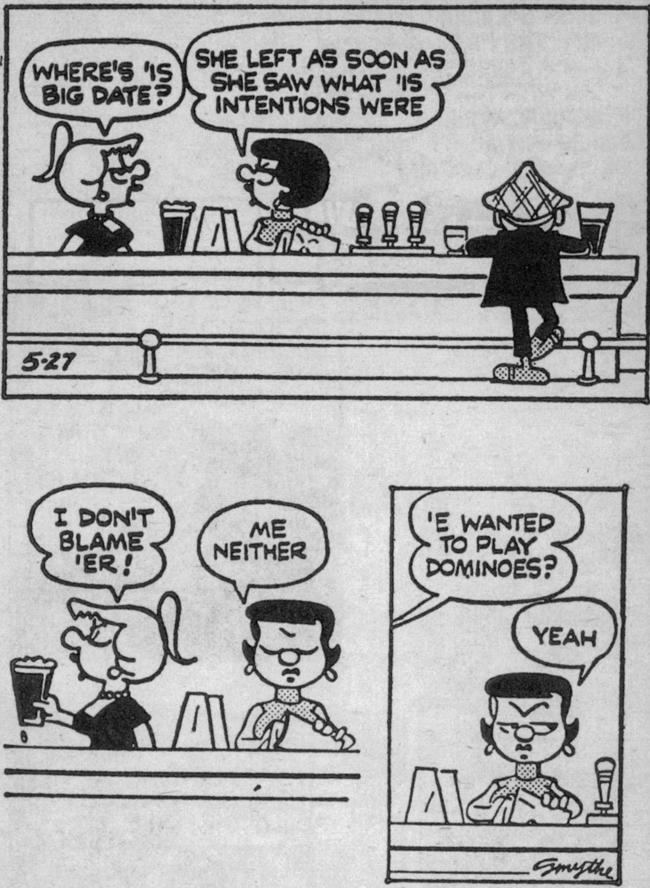
WHERE'S 'IS BIG DATE?
SHE LEFT AS SOON AS SHE SAW WHAT 'IS INTENTIONS WERE
5-27
I DON'T BLAME 'ER!
ME NEITHER
'E WANTED TO PLAY DOMINOES?
YEAH
Smythe

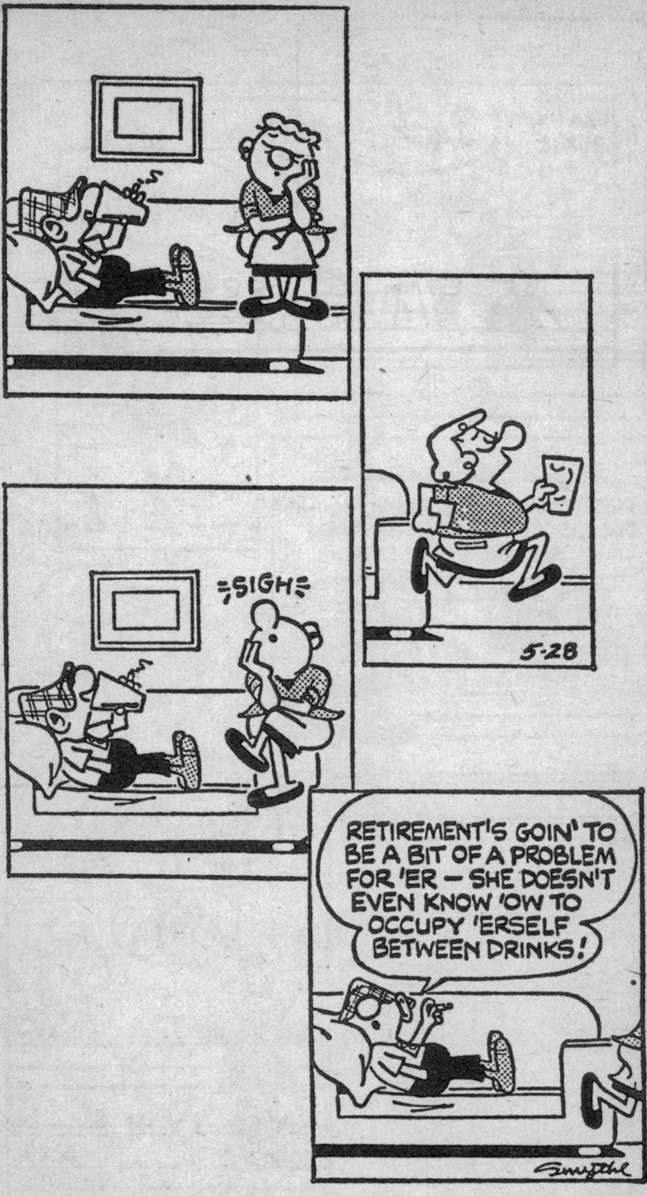

SIGH
5-28
RETIREMENT'S GOIN' TO BE A BIT OF A PROBLEM FOR 'ER — SHE DOESN'T EVEN KNOW 'OW TO OCCUPY 'ERSELF BETWEEN DRINKS!

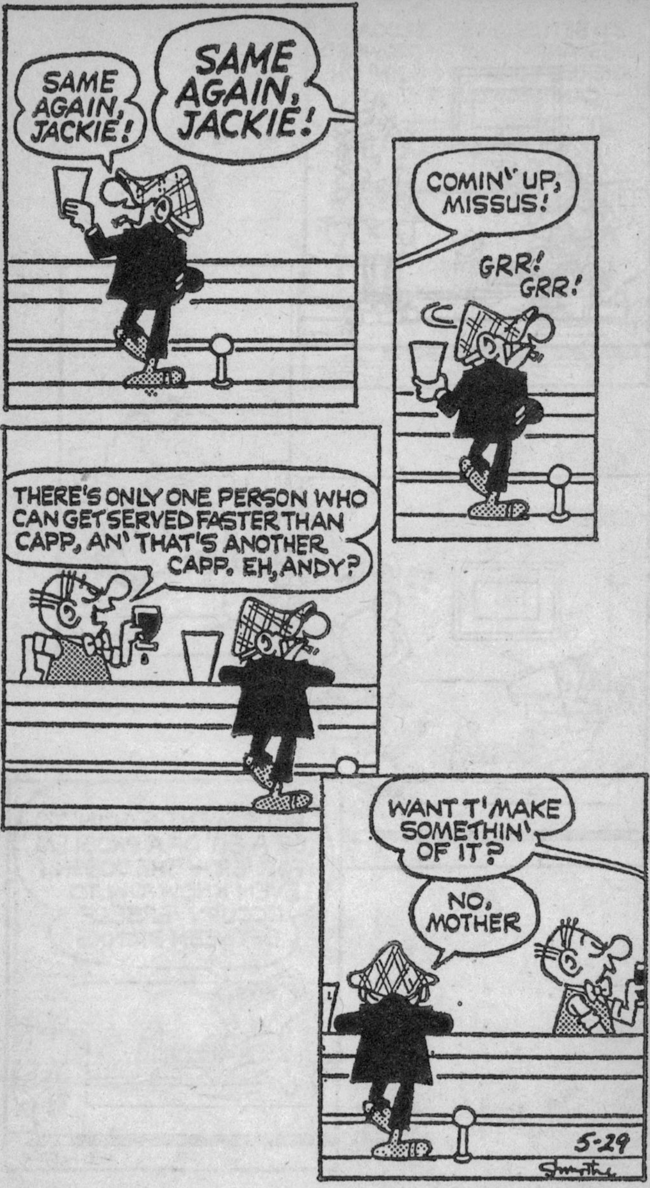
SAME AGAIN, JACKIE!
SAME AGAIN, JACKIE!
COMIN' UP, MISSUS!
GRR! GRR!
THERE'S ONLY ONE PERSON WHO CAN GET SERVED FASTER THAN CAPP, AN' THAT'S ANOTHER CAPP. EH, ANDY?
WANT T' MAKE SOMETHIN' OF IT?
NO, MOTHER
5-29
Smythe

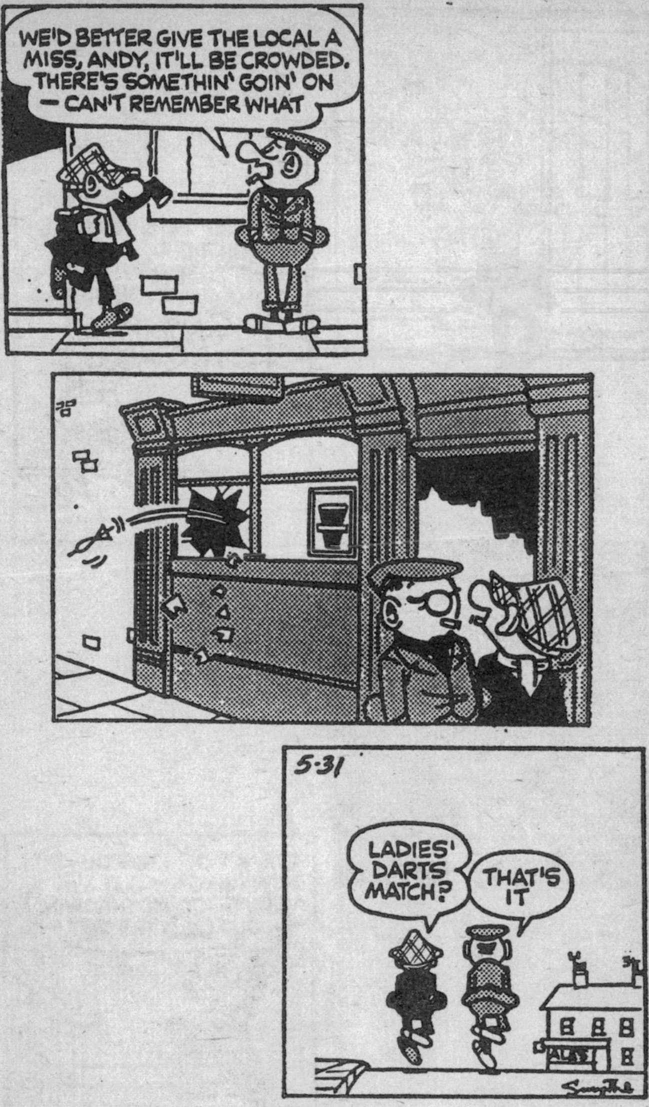
WE'D BETTER GIVE THE LOCAL A MISS, ANDY, IT'LL BE CROWDED. THERE'S SOMETHIN' GOIN' ON — CAN'T REMEMBER WHAT
5·31
LADIES' DARTS MATCH?
THAT'S IT

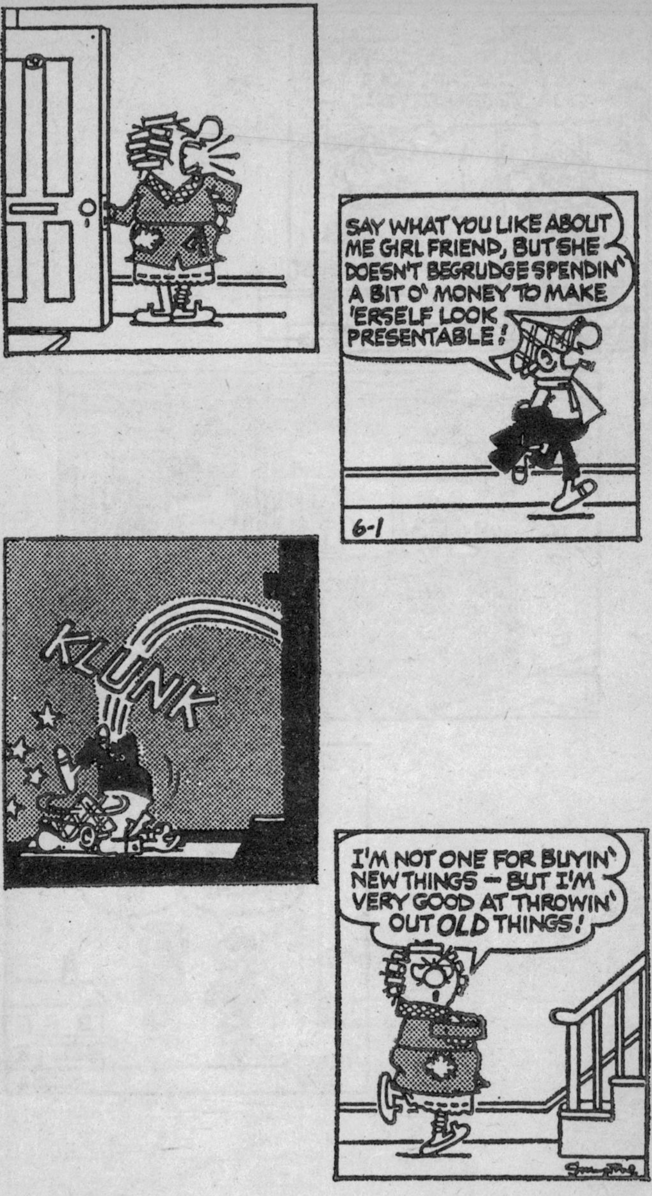
SAY WHAT YOU LIKE ABOUT ME GIRL FRIEND, BUT SHE DOESN'T BEGRUDGE SPENDIN' A BIT O' MONEY TO MAKE 'ERSELF LOOK PRESENTABLE!
6-1
KLUNK
I'M NOT ONE FOR BUYIN' NEW THINGS — BUT I'M VERY GOOD AT THROWIN' OUT OLD THINGS!

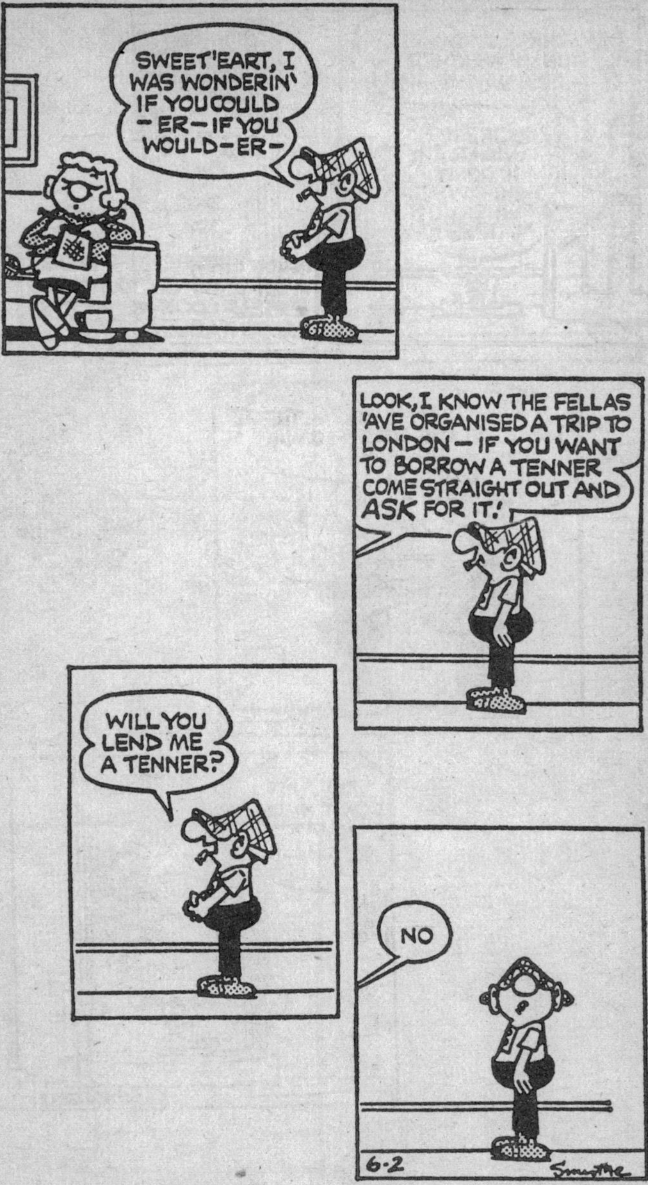
SWEET'EART, I WAS WONDERIN' IF YOU COULD — ER — IF YOU WOULD — ER —
LOOK, I KNOW THE FELLAS 'AVE ORGANISED A TRIP TO LONDON — IF YOU WANT TO BORROW A TENNER COME STRAIGHT OUT AND ASK FOR IT!
WILL YOU LEND ME A TENNER?
NO
6·2

'MORNING, ANDY. VERY FUNNY WEATHER WE'RE HAVING, EH?
SURE IS, VICAR, YOU DON'T KNOW WHERE YOU ARE—
ONE DAY IT'S WARM, THE NEXT IT'S COLD. FLO WAS ONLY SAYIN'—
YOU JUST DON'T KNOW *WHAT* TO PAWN
6-3

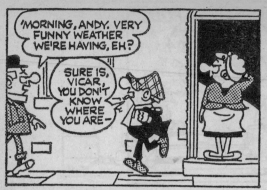

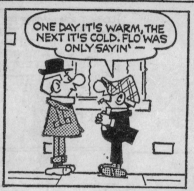

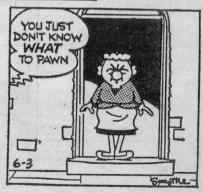

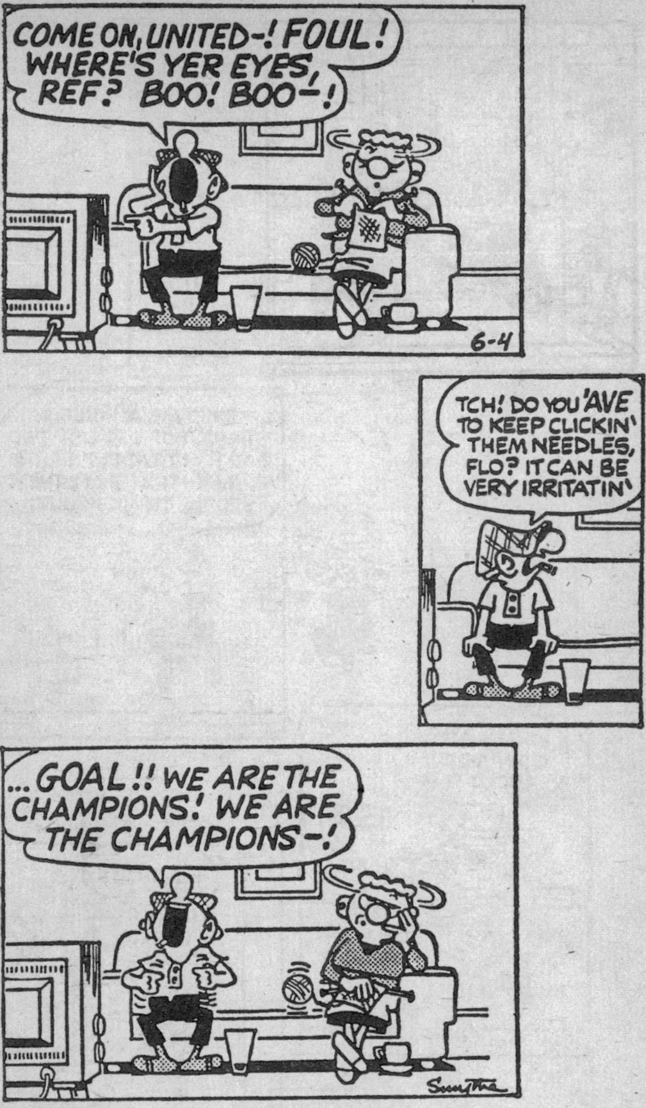
COME ON, UNITED-! FOUL! WHERE'S YER EYES, REF? BOO! BOO-!
6-4
TCH! DO YOU 'AVE TO KEEP CLICKIN' THEM NEEDLES, FLO? IT CAN BE VERY IRRITATIN'
...GOAL!! WE ARE THE CHAMPIONS! WE ARE THE CHAMPIONS-!

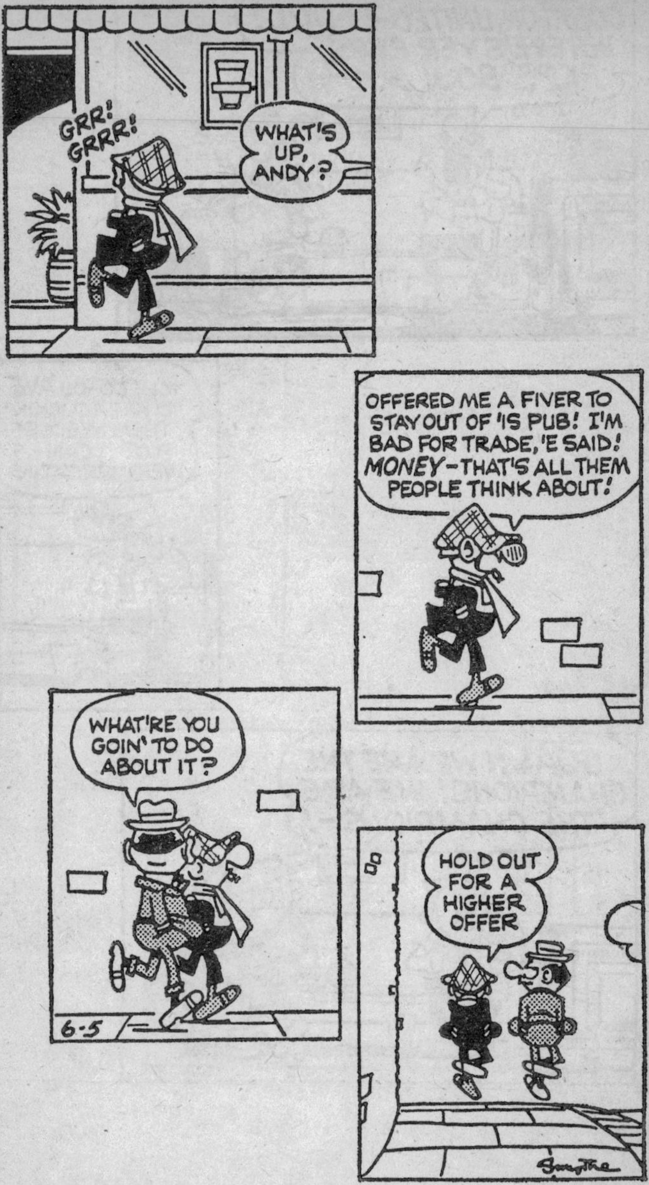
GRR! GRRR!
WHAT'S UP, ANDY?
OFFERED ME A FIVER TO STAY OUT OF 'IS PUB! I'M BAD FOR TRADE, 'E SAID! MONEY – THAT'S ALL THEM PEOPLE THINK ABOUT!
WHAT'RE YOU GOIN' TO DO ABOUT IT?
HOLD OUT FOR A HIGHER OFFER
6-5
Smythe

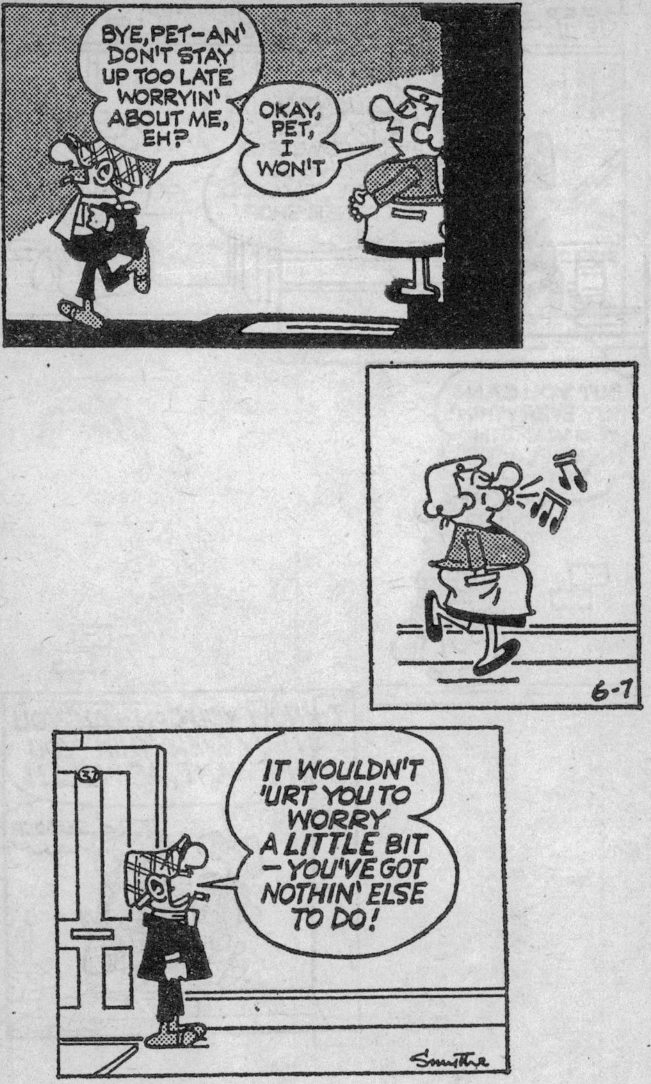
BYE, PET—AN' DON'T STAY UP TOO LATE WORRYIN' ABOUT ME, EH?
OKAY, PET, I WON'T
6-7
IT WOULDN'T 'URT YOU TO WORRY A *LITTLE* BIT —YOU'VE GOT NOTHIN' ELSE TO DO!
Smythe

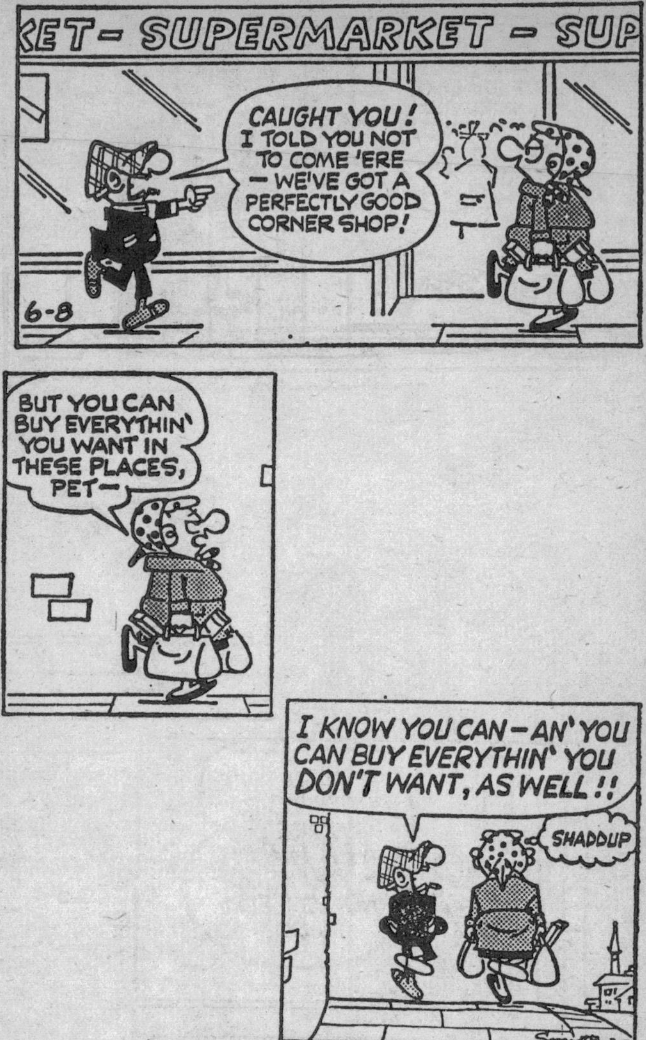
KET- SUPERMARKET - SUP
CAUGHT YOU! I TOLD YOU NOT TO COME 'ERE — WE'VE GOT A PERFECTLY GOOD CORNER SHOP!
6-8
BUT YOU CAN BUY EVERYTHIN' YOU WANT IN THESE PLACES, PET—
I KNOW YOU CAN—AN' YOU CAN BUY EVERYTHIN' YOU DON'T WANT, AS WELL!!
SHADDUP
Smythe

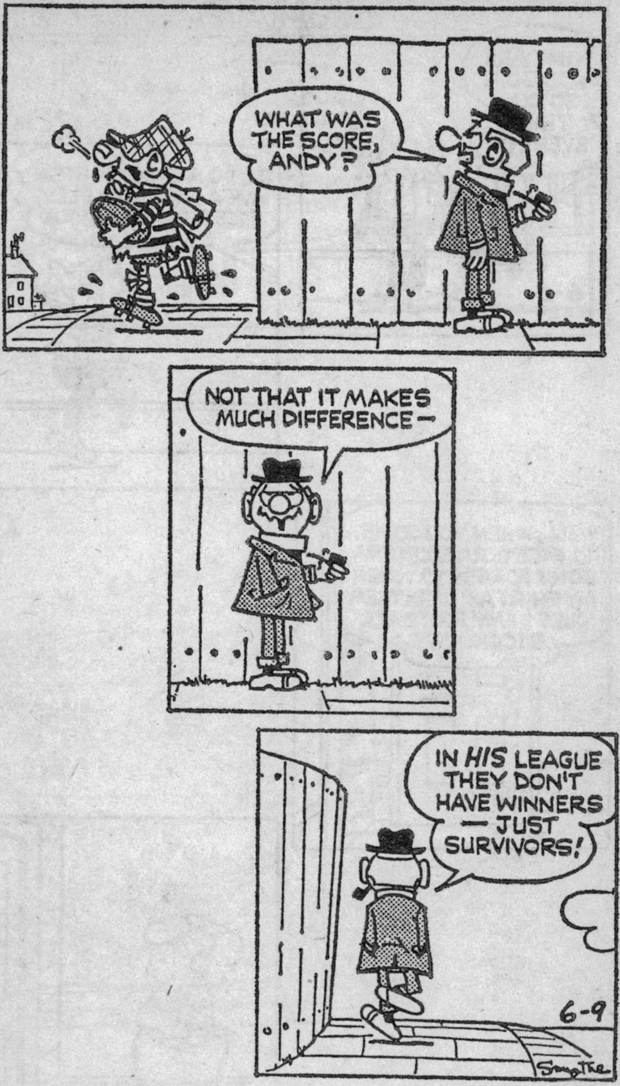
WHAT WAS THE SCORE, ANDY?
NOT THAT IT MAKES MUCH DIFFERENCE—
IN HIS LEAGUE THEY DON'T HAVE WINNERS — JUST SURVIVORS!
6-9
Smythe

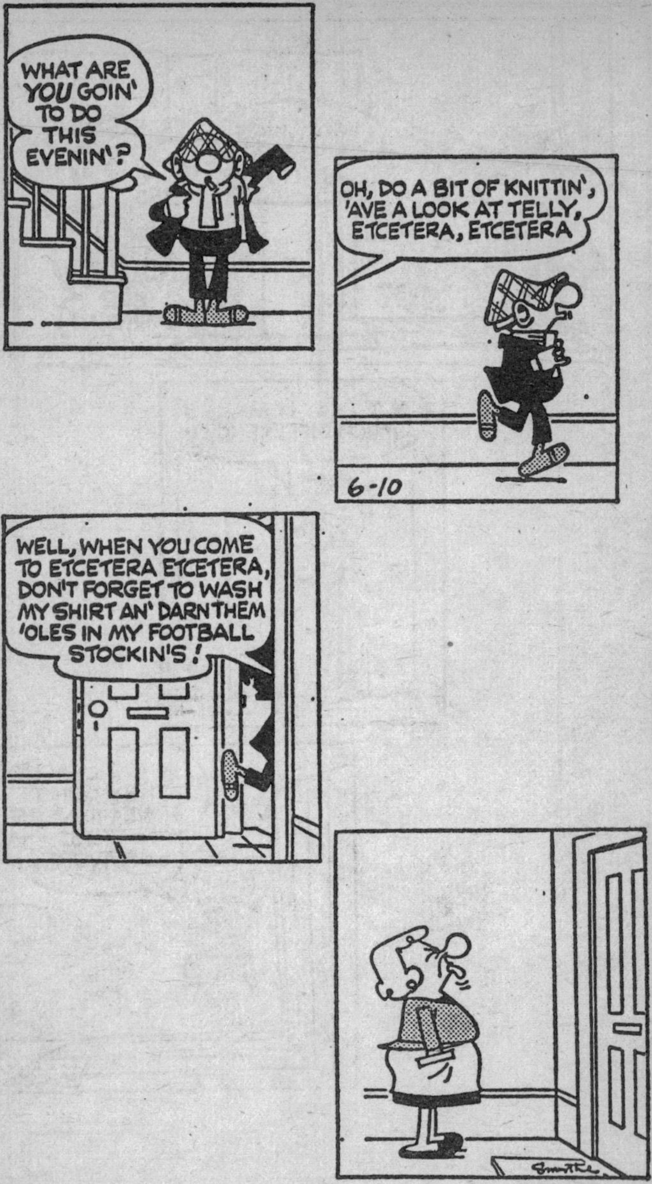
WHAT ARE YOU GOIN' TO DO THIS EVENIN'?
OH, DO A BIT OF KNITTIN', 'AVE A LOOK AT TELLY, ETCETERA, ETCETERA
6-10
WELL, WHEN YOU COME TO ETCETERA ETCETERA, DON'T FORGET TO WASH MY SHIRT AN' DARN THEM 'OLES IN MY FOOTBALL STOCKIN'S!
Smythe

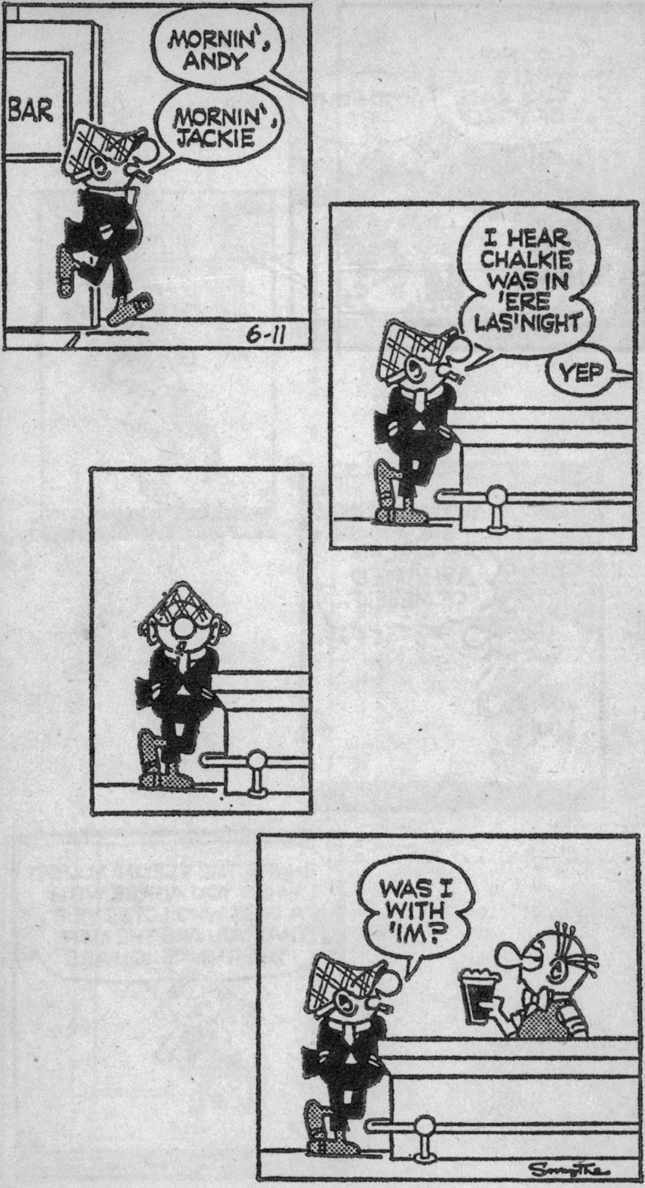

BAR
MORNIN', ANDY
MORNIN', JACKIE
6-11
I HEAR CHALKIE WAS IN 'ERE LAS'NIGHT
YEP
WAS I WITH 'IM?
Smythe

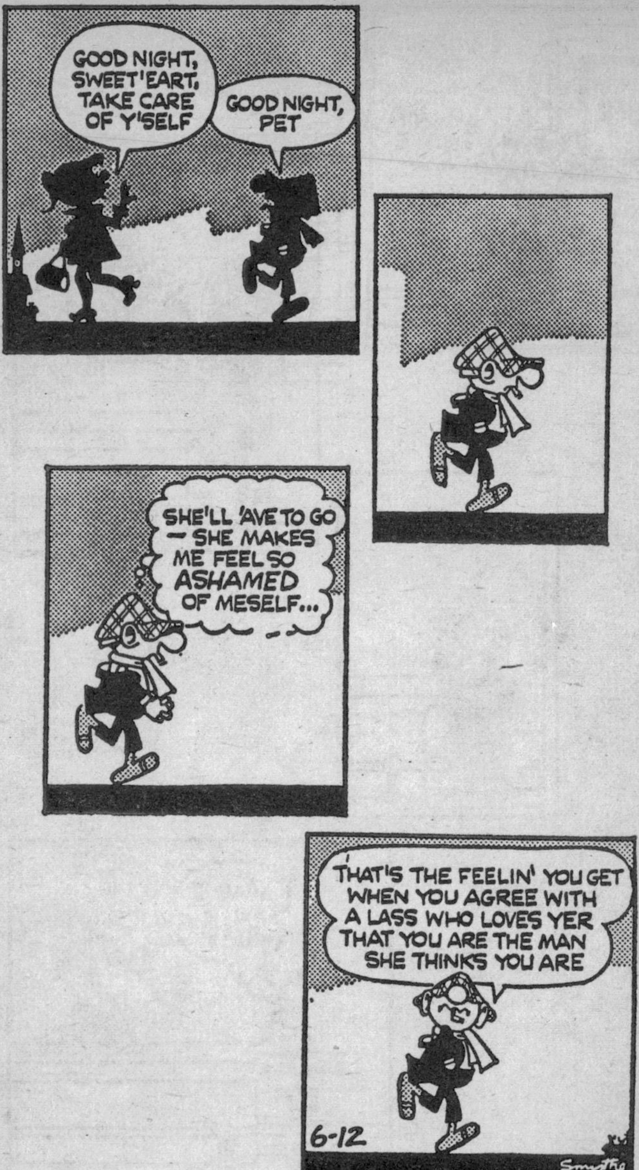
GOOD NIGHT, SWEET'EART, TAKE CARE OF Y'SELF
GOOD NIGHT, PET
SHE'LL 'AVE TO GO — SHE MAKES ME FEEL SO ASHAMED OF MESELF...
THAT'S THE FEELIN' YOU GET WHEN YOU AGREE WITH A LASS WHO LOVES YER THAT YOU ARE THE MAN SHE THINKS YOU ARE
6-12
Smythe

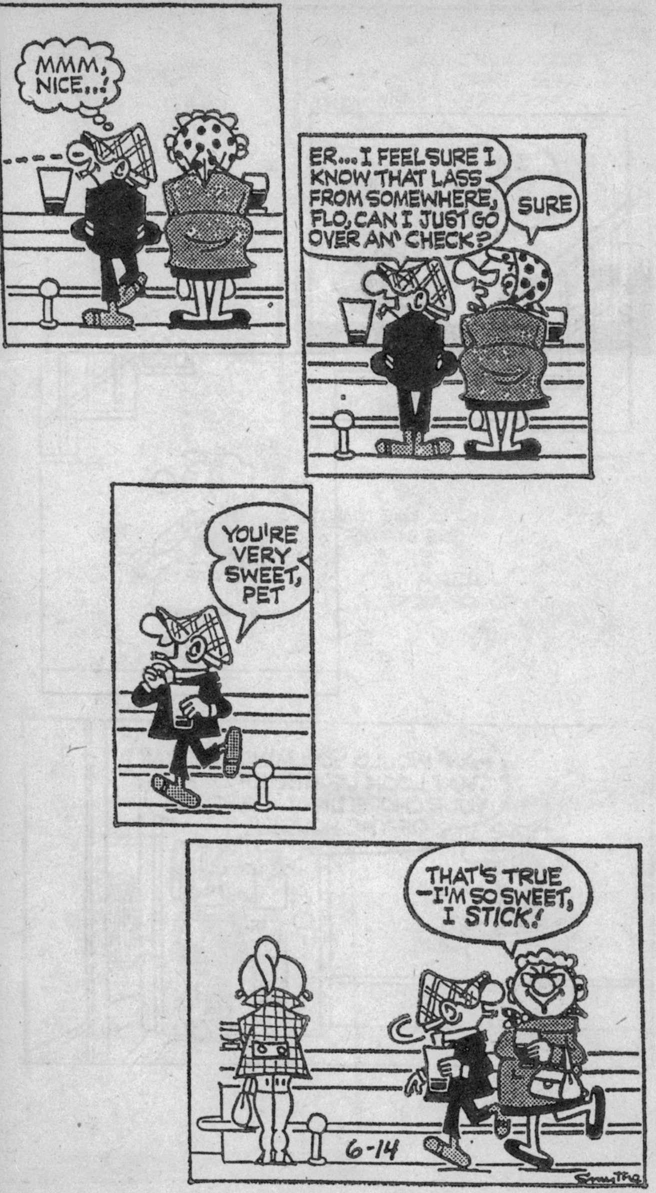

MMM, NICE...!
ER...I FEEL SURE I KNOW THAT LASS FROM SOMEWHERE, FLO, CAN I JUST GO OVER AN' CHECK?
SURE
YOU'RE VERY SWEET, PET
THAT'S TRUE —I'M SO SWEET, I STICK!
6-14
Smythe

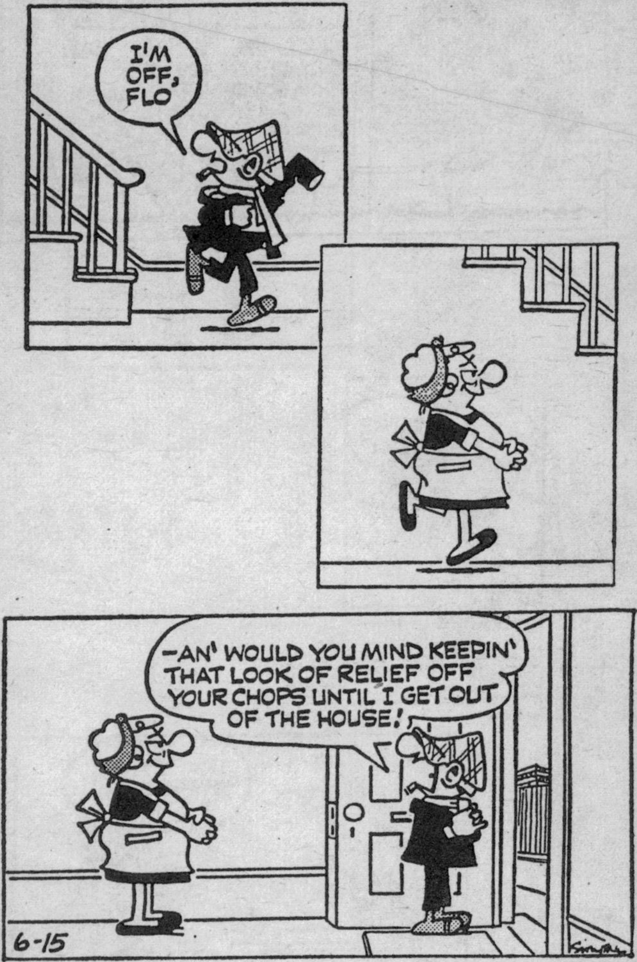
I'M OFF, FLO
—AN' WOULD YOU MIND KEEPIN' THAT LOOK OF RELIEF OFF YOUR CHOPS UNTIL I GET OUT OF THE HOUSE!
6-15

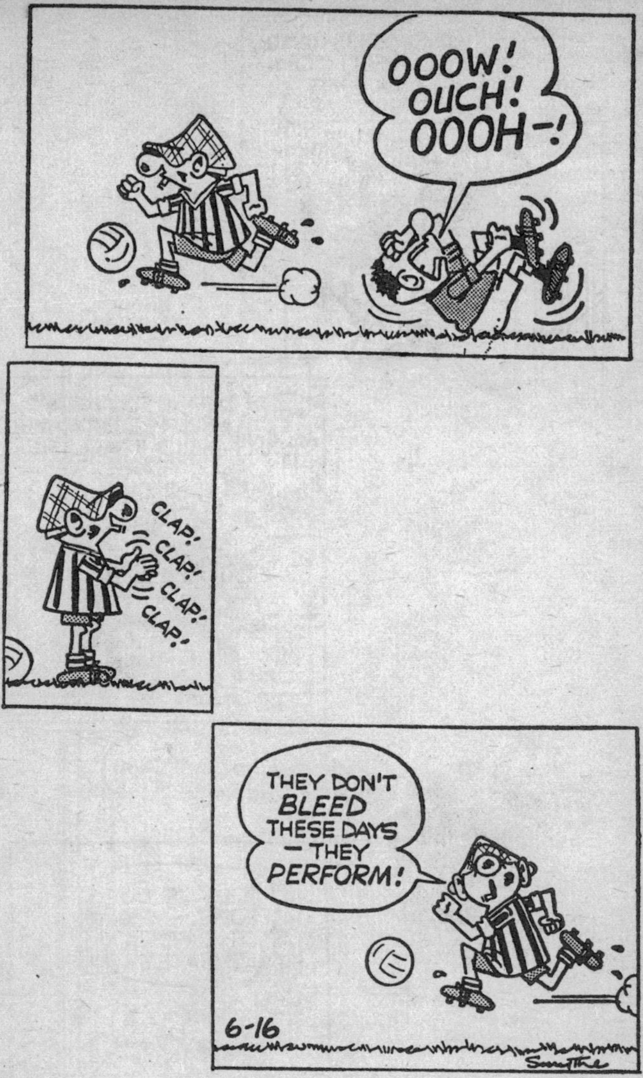
OOOW! OUCH! OOOH–!
CLAP! CLAP! CLAP! CLAP!
THEY DON'T *BLEED* THESE DAYS – THEY *PERFORM!*
6-16
Smythe

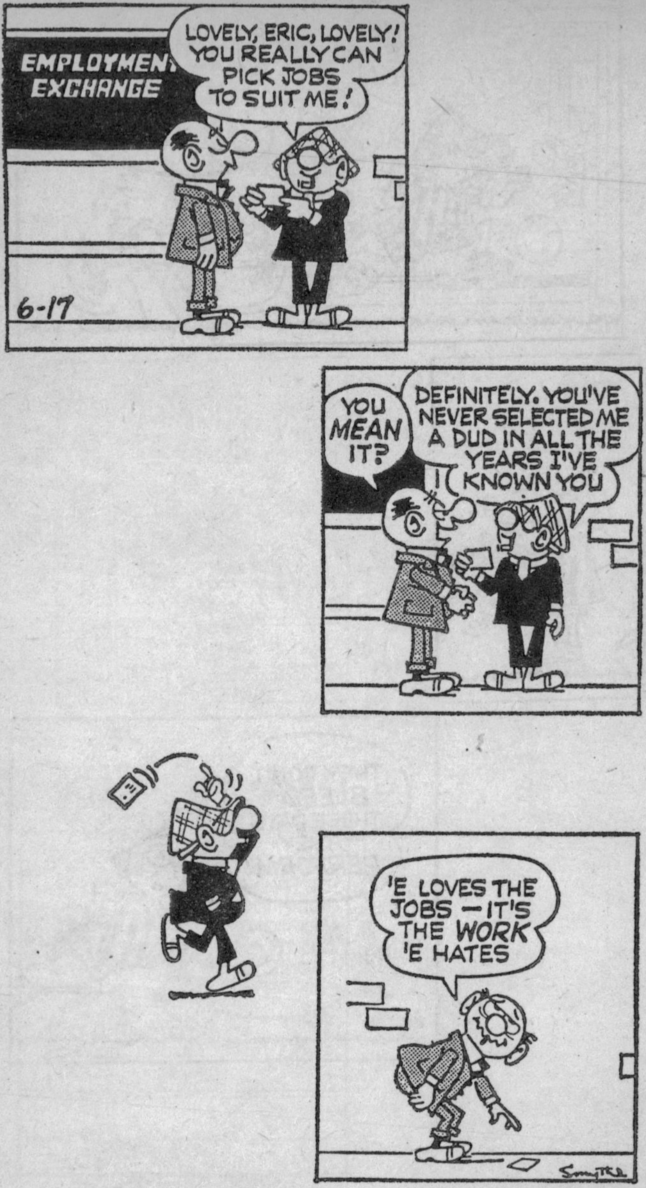
EMPLOYMENT EXCHANGE
LOVELY, ERIC, LOVELY! YOU REALLY CAN PICK JOBS TO SUIT ME!
6-17
YOU MEAN IT?
DEFINITELY. YOU'VE NEVER SELECTED ME A DUD IN ALL THE YEARS I'VE KNOWN YOU
'E LOVES THE JOBS — IT'S THE WORK 'E HATES

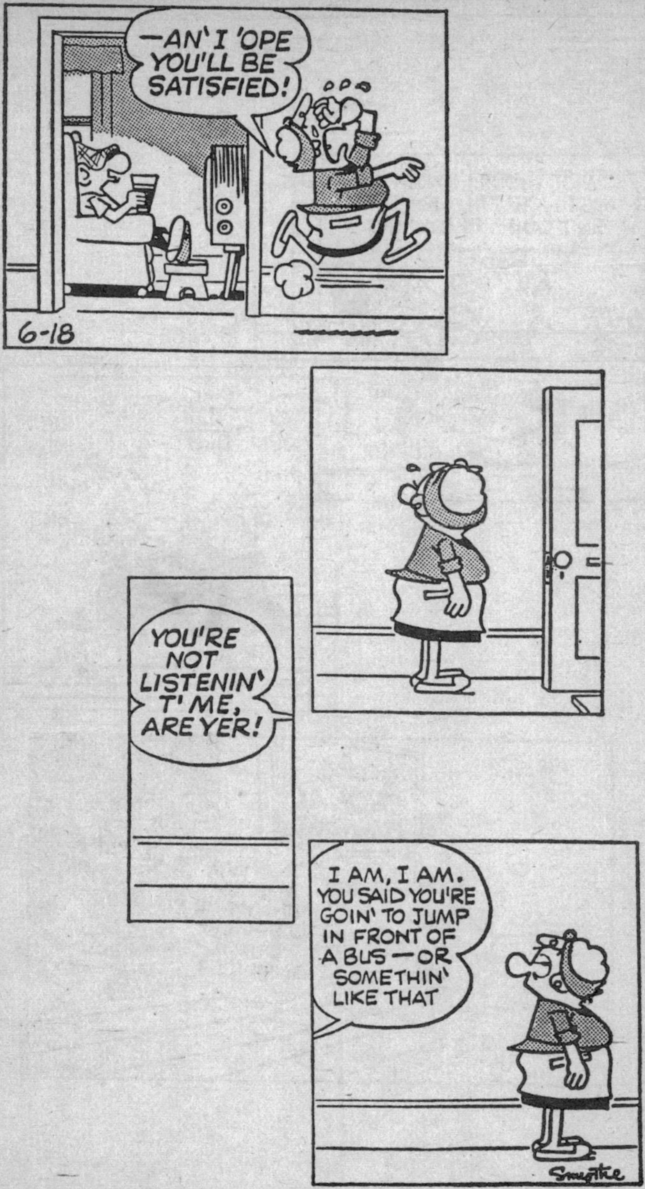
—AN' I 'OPE YOU'LL BE SATISFIED!
6-18
YOU'RE NOT LISTENIN' T' ME, ARE YER!
I AM, I AM. YOU SAID YOU'RE GOIN' TO JUMP IN FRONT OF A BUS—OR SOMETHIN' LIKE THAT
Smythe

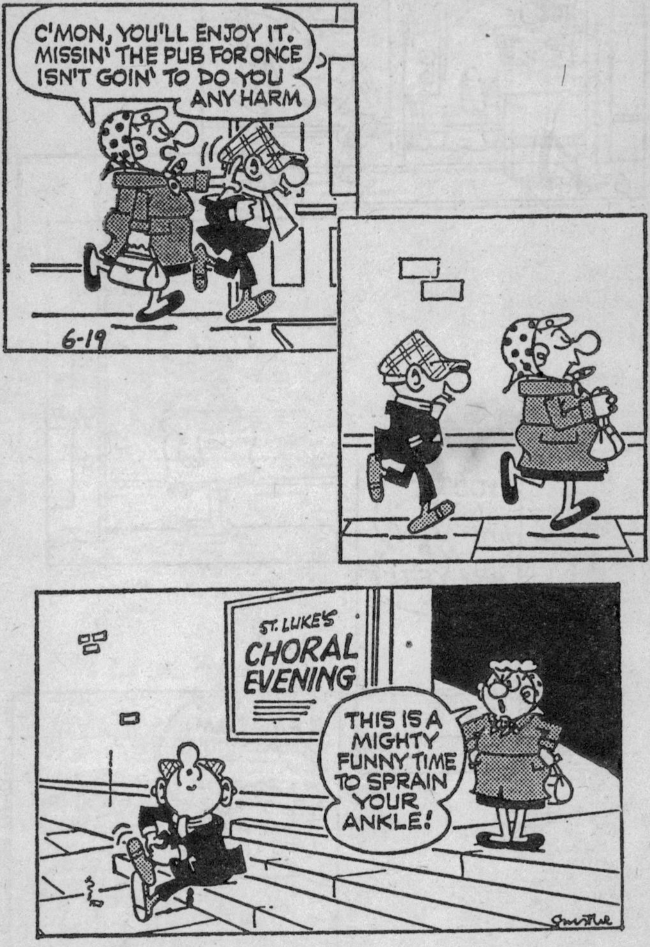
C'MON, YOU'LL ENJOY IT. MISSIN' THE PUB FOR ONCE ISN'T GOIN' TO DO YOU ANY HARM
6-19
ST. LUKE'S
CHORAL EVENING
THIS IS A MIGHTY FUNNY TIME TO SPRAIN YOUR ANKLE!
Smythe

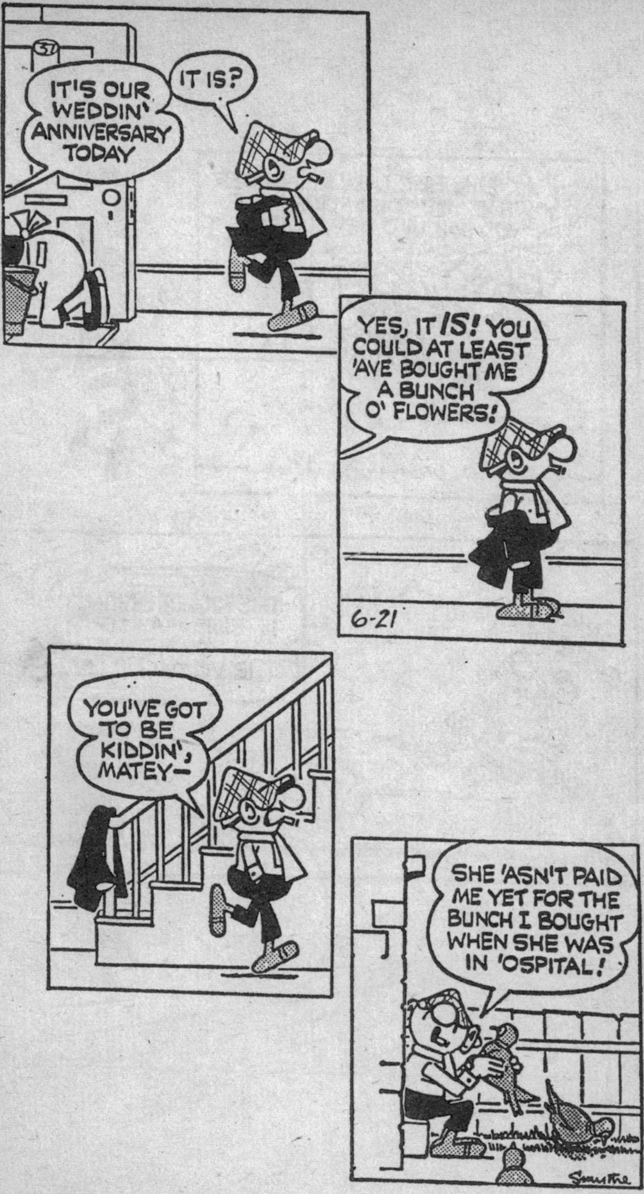
IT'S OUR WEDDIN' ANNIVERSARY TODAY
IT IS?
YES, IT IS! YOU COULD AT LEAST 'AVE BOUGHT ME A BUNCH O' FLOWERS!
6-21
YOU'VE GOT TO BE KIDDIN', MATEY—
SHE 'ASN'T PAID ME YET FOR THE BUNCH I BOUGHT WHEN SHE WAS IN 'OSPITAL!
Smythe

AT 'EM, ERIC, LAD! REMEMBER WHAT YOU TOLD YOURSELF YOU SHOULD DEVELOP....
GRR! GRR!
CRUNCH
GRR! GRRR!
THE KILLER INSTINCT IS FINE — AS LONG AS YOU'RE NOT THE VICTIM OF IT!
6-22
Smythe

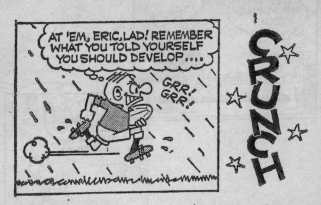

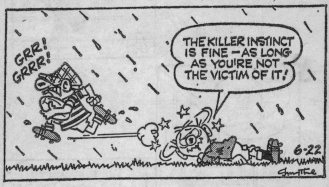

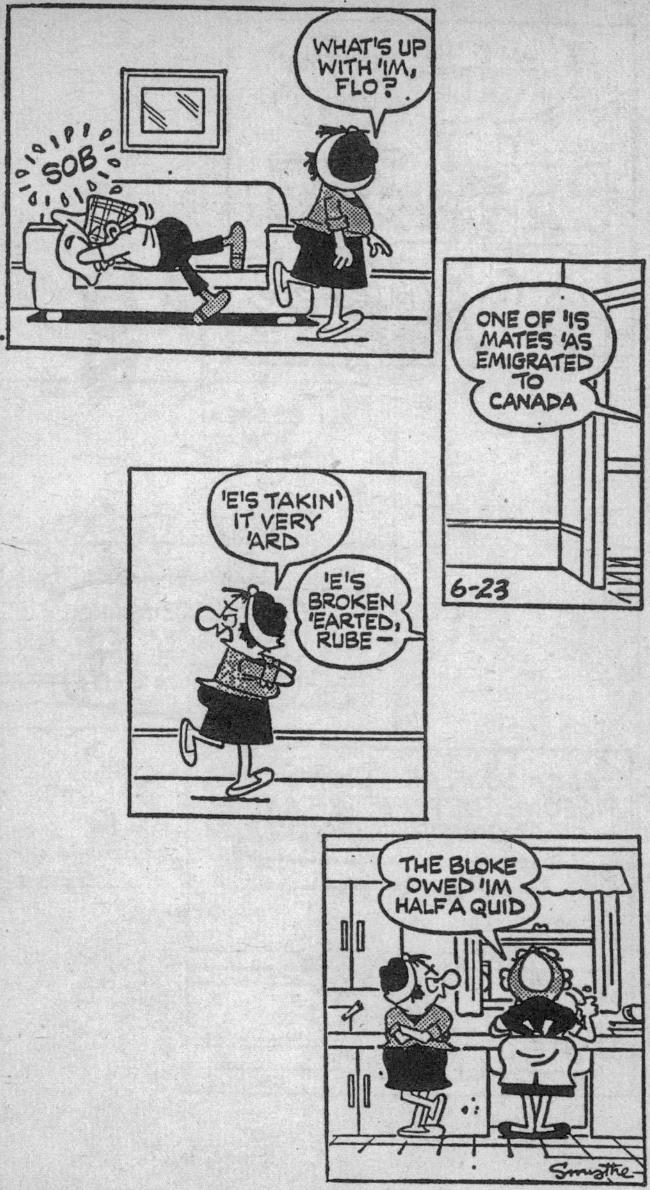
WHAT'S UP WITH 'IM, FLO?
SOB
ONE OF 'IS MATES 'AS EMIGRATED TO CANADA
6-23
'E'S TAKIN' IT VERY 'ARD
'E'S BROKEN 'EARTED, RUBE—
THE BLOKE OWED 'IM HALF A QUID
Smythe

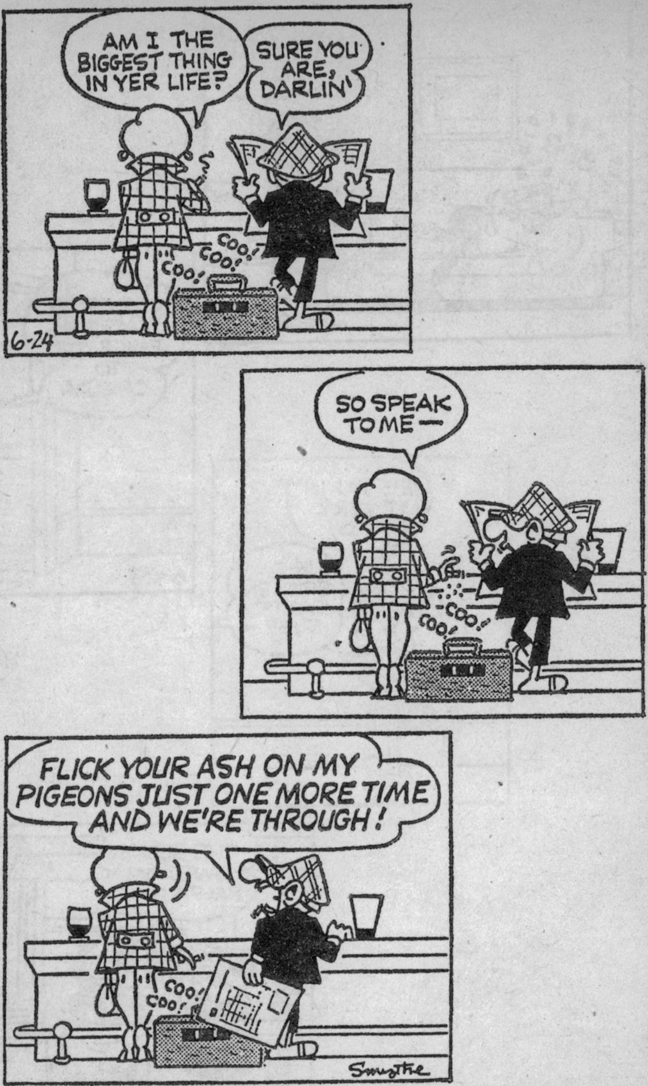

6-24
AM I THE BIGGEST THING IN YER LIFE?
SURE YOU ARE, DARLIN'
COO! COO! COO!
SO SPEAK TO ME —
COO! COO!
FLICK YOUR ASH ON MY PIGEONS JUST ONE MORE TIME AND WE'RE THROUGH!
COO! COO!
Smythe

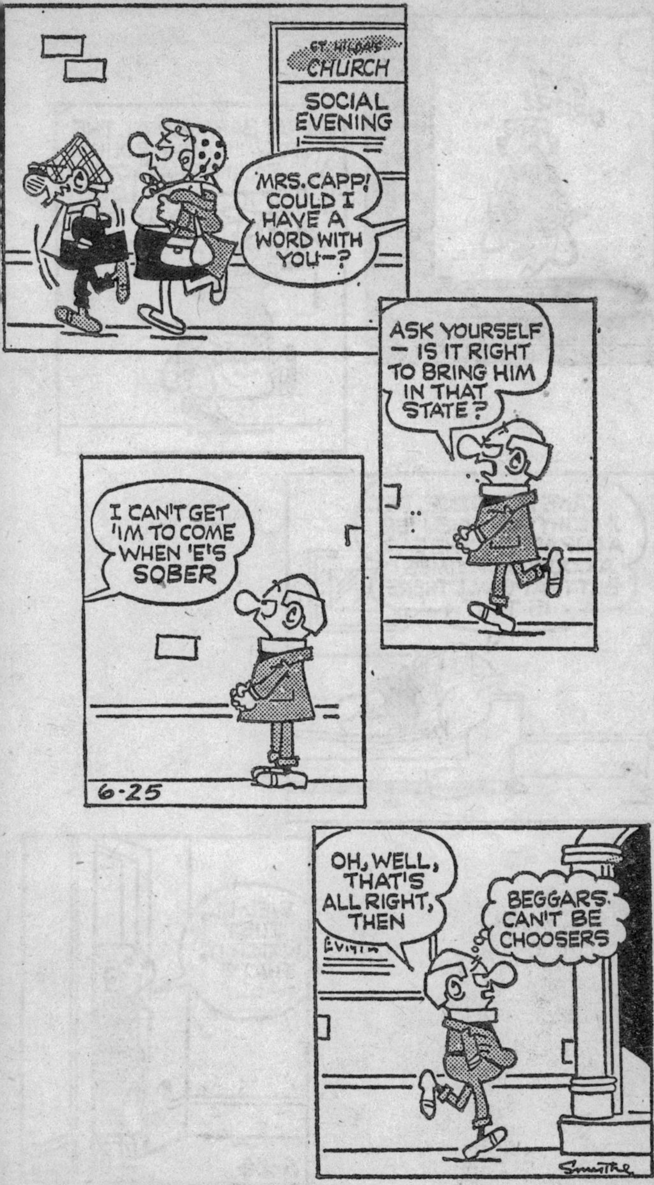
CHURCH
SOCIAL EVENING
MRS. CAPP! COULD I HAVE A WORD WITH YOU—?
ASK YOURSELF — IS IT RIGHT TO BRING HIM IN THAT STATE?
I CAN'T GET 'IM TO COME WHEN 'E'S SOBER
6-25
OH, WELL, THAT'S ALL RIGHT, THEN
BEGGARS CAN'T BE CHOOSERS
Smythe

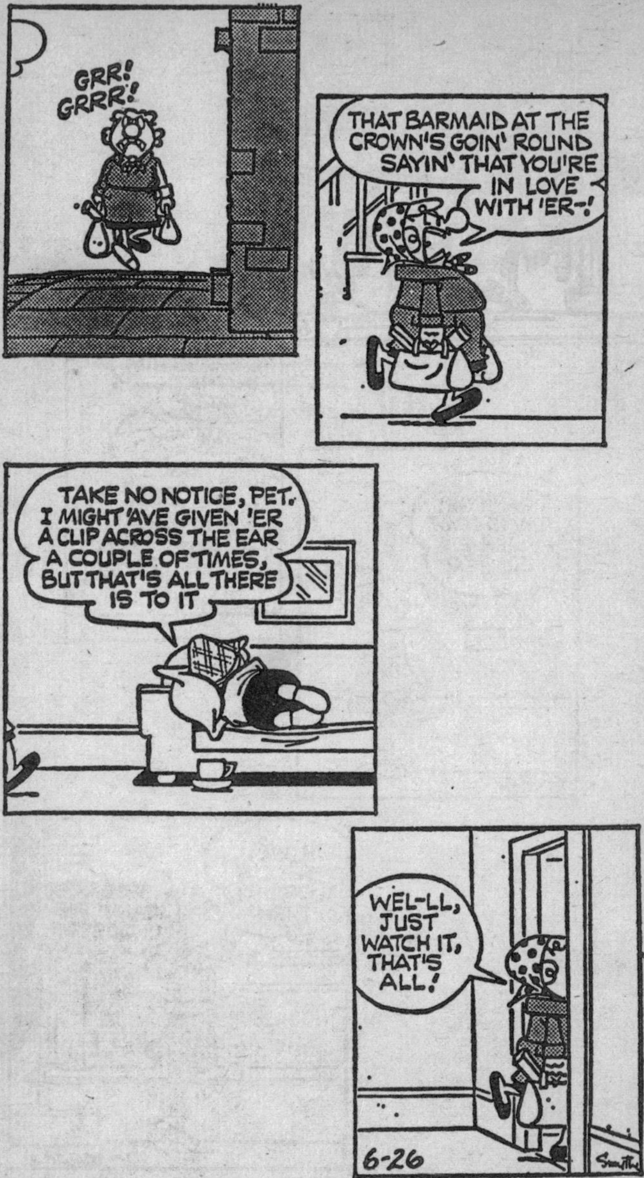
GRR! GRRR!
THAT BARMAID AT THE CROWN'S GOIN' ROUND SAYIN' THAT YOU'RE IN LOVE WITH 'ER-!
TAKE NO NOTICE, PET. I MIGHT 'AVE GIVEN 'ER A CLIP ACROSS THE EAR A COUPLE OF TIMES, BUT THAT'S ALL THERE IS TO IT
WEL-LL, JUST WATCH IT, THAT'S ALL!
6-26
Smythe

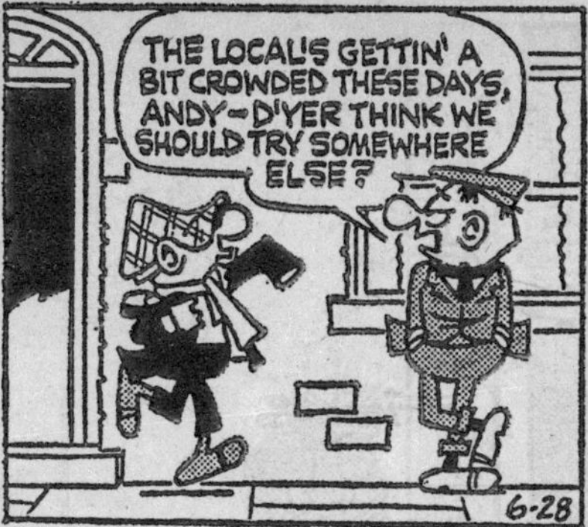
THE LOCAL'S GETTIN' A BIT CROWDED THESE DAYS, ANDY—D'YER THINK WE SHOULD TRY SOMEWHERE ELSE?
6-28

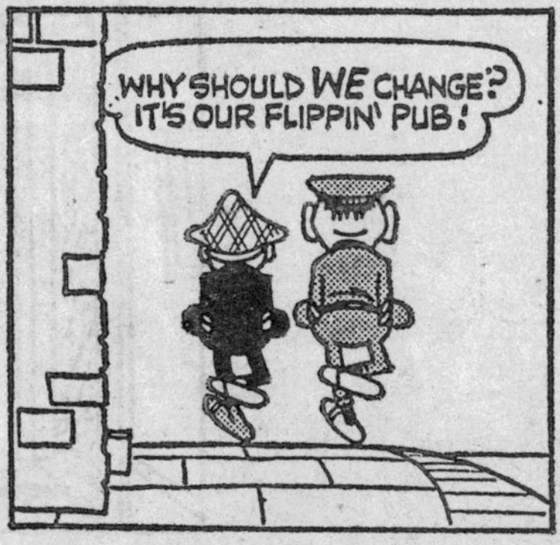
WHY SHOULD WE CHANGE? IT'S OUR FLIPPIN' PUB!

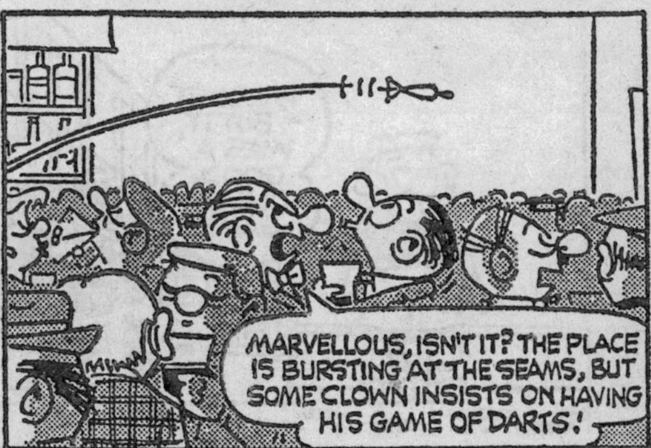
MARVELLOUS, ISN'T IT? THE PLACE IS BURSTING AT THE SEAMS, BUT SOME CLOWN INSISTS ON HAVING HIS GAME OF DARTS!

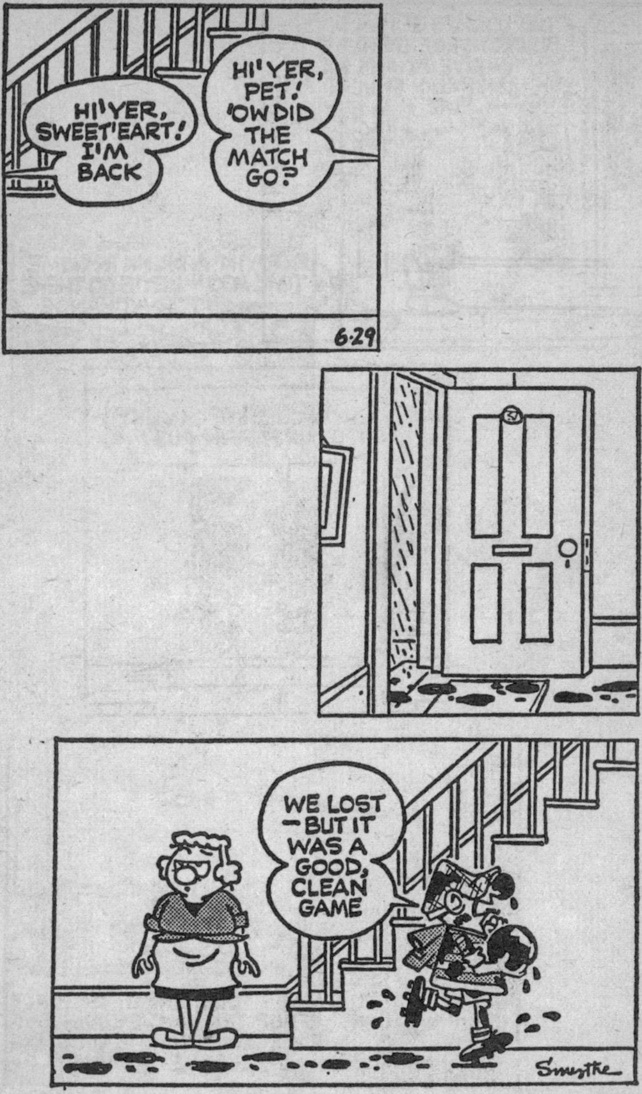
HI'YER, SWEET'EART! I'M BACK
HI'YER, PET! 'OW DID THE MATCH GO?
6.29
WE LOST —BUT IT WAS A GOOD, CLEAN GAME
Smythe

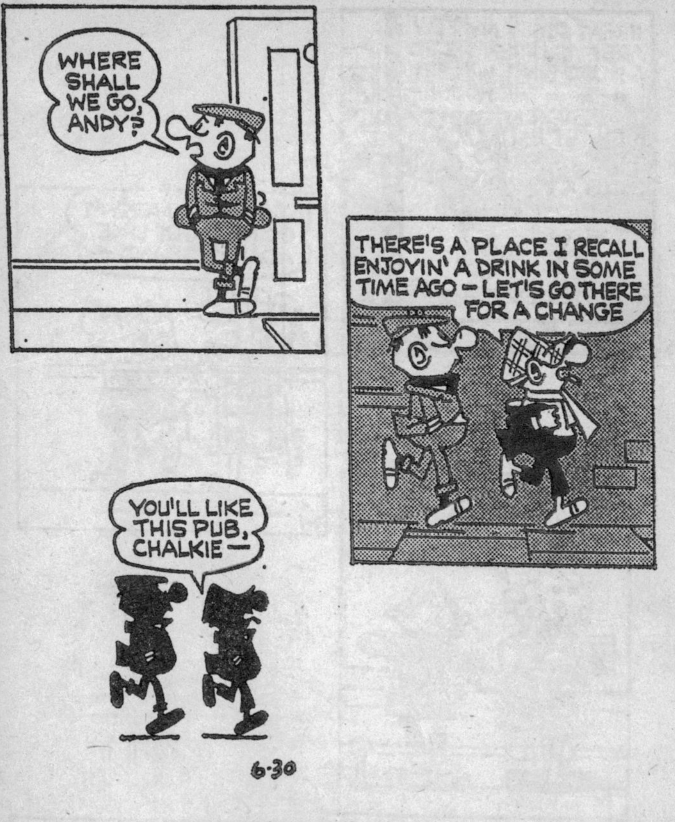
WHERE SHALL WE GO, ANDY?
THERE'S A PLACE I RECALL ENJOYIN' A DRINK IN SOME TIME AGO — LET'S GO THERE FOR A CHANGE
YOU'LL LIKE THIS PUB, CHALKIE —
6-30
THEY'VE GOT A SPECIAL ATTRACTION — NO JUKE BOX!
ALES

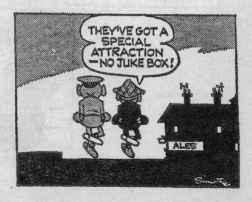

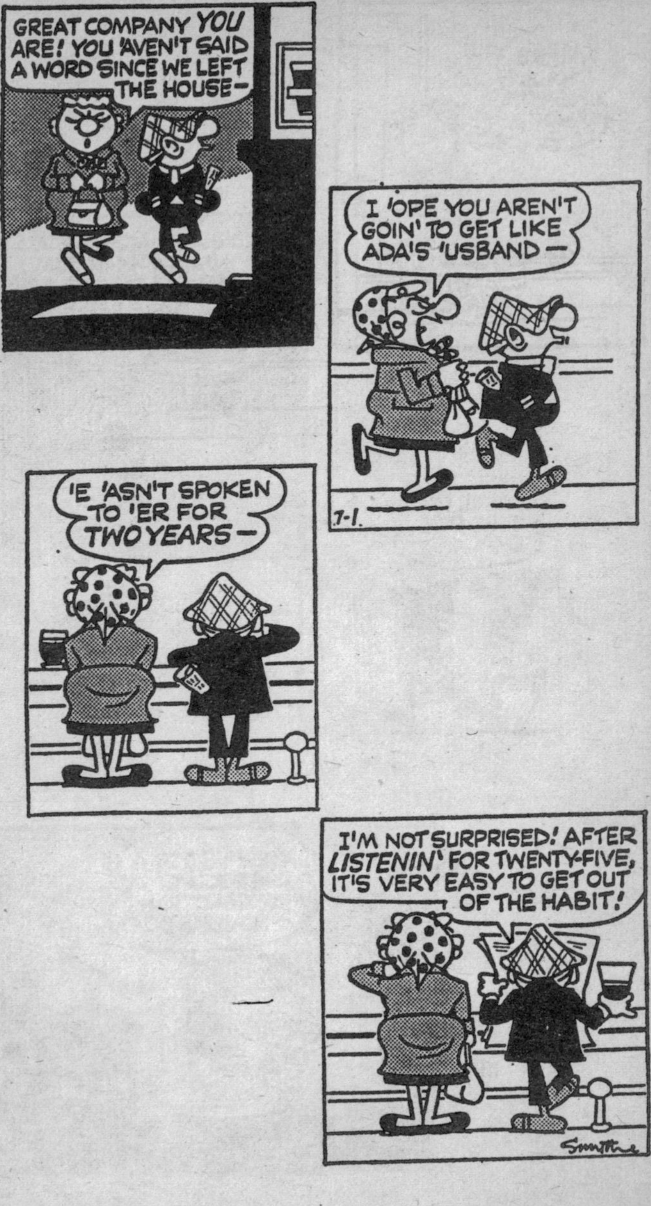
GREAT COMPANY YOU ARE! YOU 'AVEN'T SAID A WORD SINCE WE LEFT THE HOUSE—
I 'OPE YOU AREN'T GOIN' TO GET LIKE ADA'S 'USBAND—
7-1.
'E 'ASN'T SPOKEN TO 'ER FOR TWO YEARS—
I'M NOT SURPRISED! AFTER LISTENIN' FOR TWENTY-FIVE, IT'S VERY EASY TO GET OUT OF THE HABIT!
Smythe

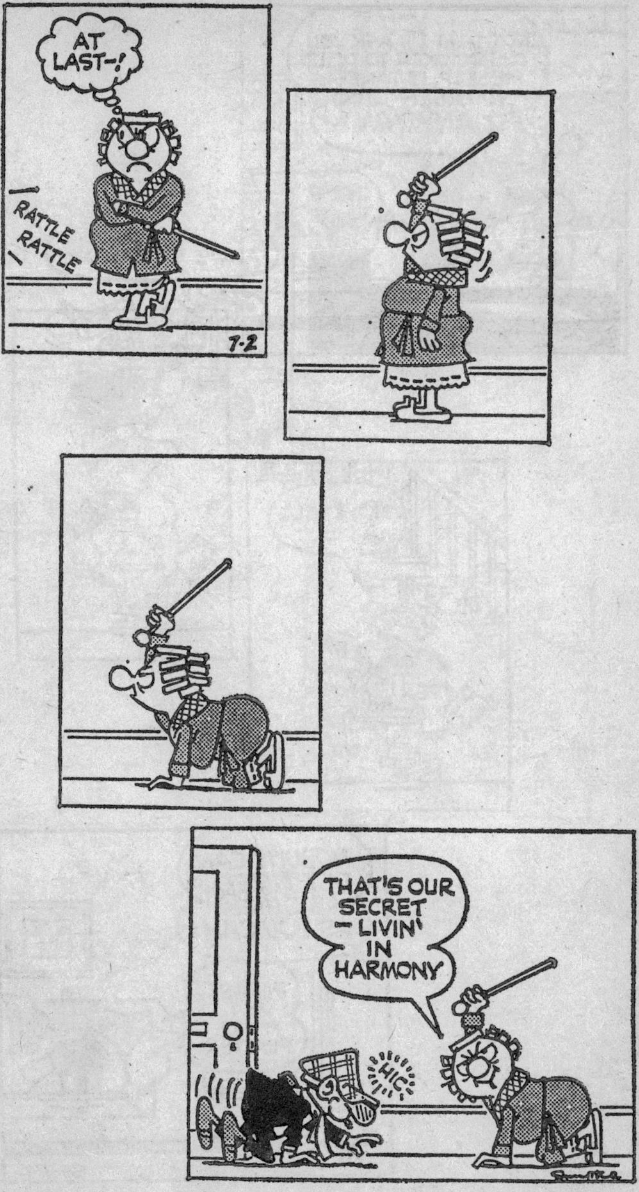
AT LAST-!
RATTLE RATTLE
7-2
THAT'S OUR SECRET - LIVIN' IN HARMONY
HIC

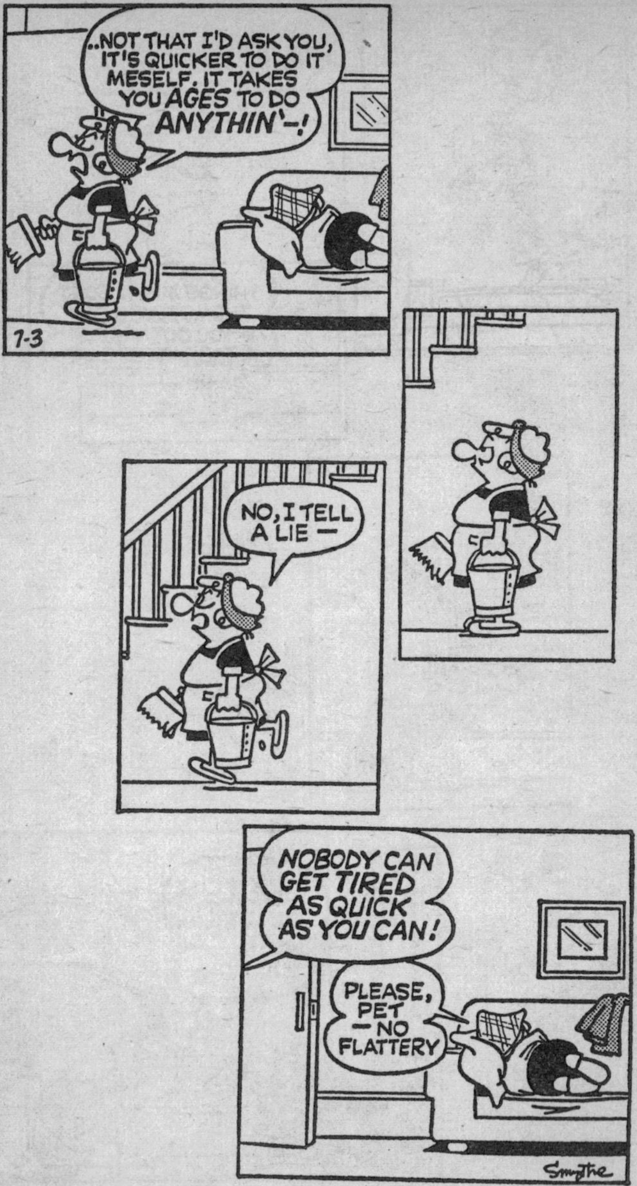
..NOT THAT I'D ASK YOU, IT'S QUICKER TO DO IT MESELF. IT TAKES YOU AGES TO DO ANYTHIN'–!
7-3
NO, I TELL A LIE –
NOBODY CAN GET TIRED AS QUICK AS YOU CAN!
PLEASE, PET – NO FLATTERY
Smythe

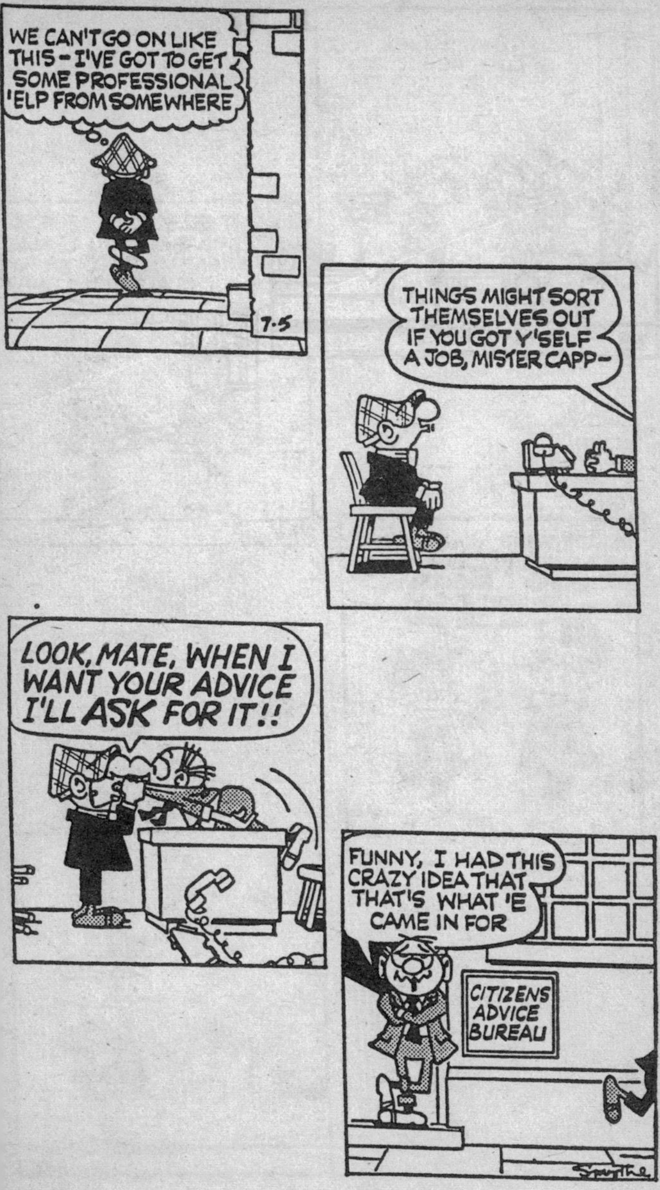
WE CAN'T GO ON LIKE THIS - I'VE GOT TO GET SOME PROFESSIONAL 'ELP FROM SOMEWHERE
7-5
THINGS MIGHT SORT THEMSELVES OUT IF YOU GOT Y'SELF A JOB, MISTER CAPP-
LOOK, MATE, WHEN I WANT YOUR ADVICE I'LL ASK FOR IT!!
FUNNY, I HAD THIS CRAZY IDEA THAT THAT'S WHAT 'E CAME IN FOR
CITIZENS ADVICE BUREAU
Smythe

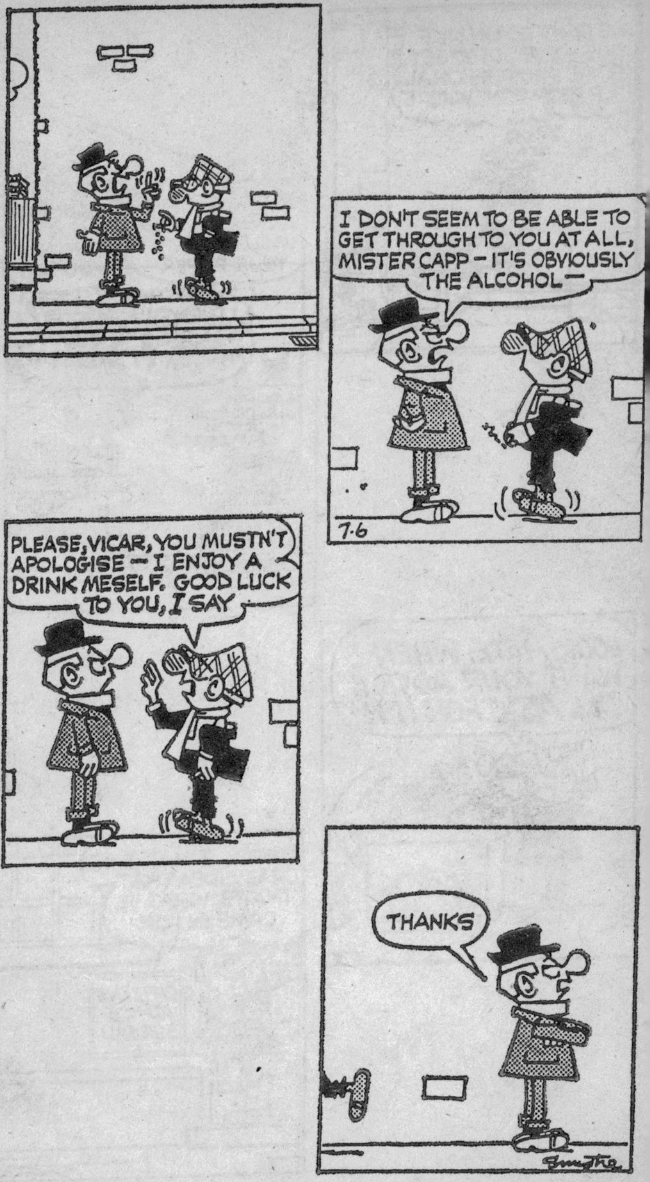
I DON'T SEEM TO BE ABLE TO GET THROUGH TO YOU AT ALL, MISTER CAPP – IT'S OBVIOUSLY THE ALCOHOL –
PLEASE, VICAR, YOU MUSTN'T APOLOGISE – I ENJOY A DRINK MESELF. GOOD LUCK TO YOU, I SAY
THANKS

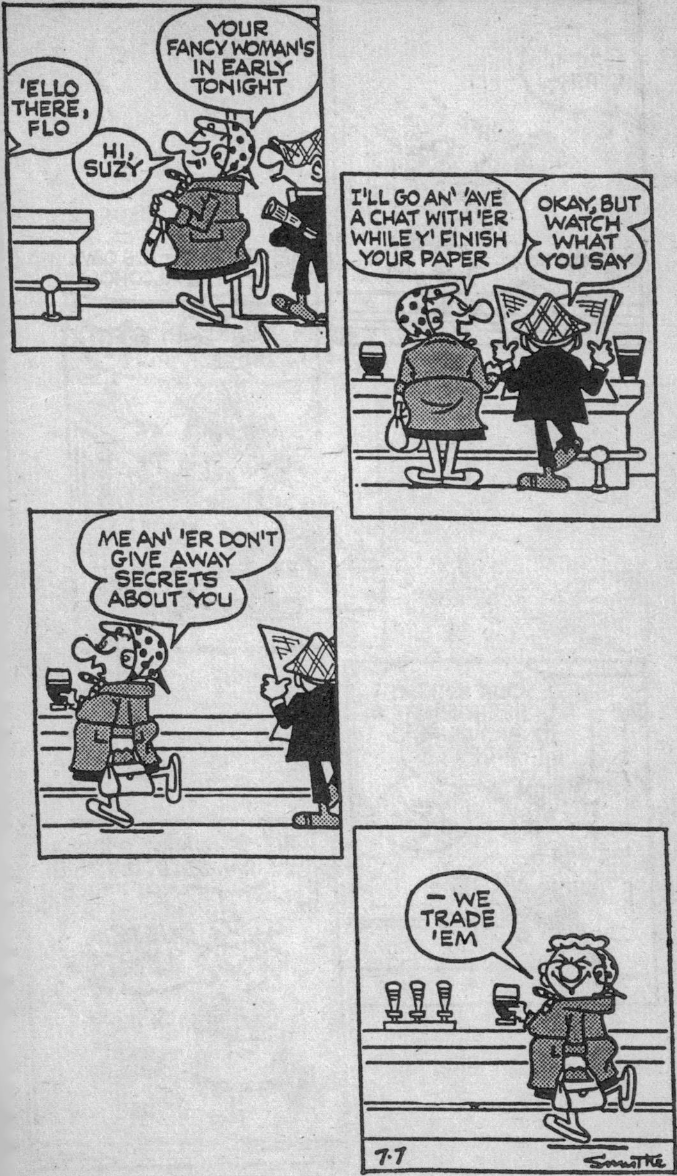
YOUR FANCY WOMAN'S IN EARLY TONIGHT
'ELLO THERE, FLO
HI, SUZY
I'LL GO AN' 'AVE A CHAT WITH 'ER WHILE Y' FINISH YOUR PAPER
OKAY, BUT WATCH WHAT YOU SAY
ME AN' 'ER DON'T GIVE AWAY SECRETS ABOUT YOU
— WE TRADE 'EM
7·7
Smythe

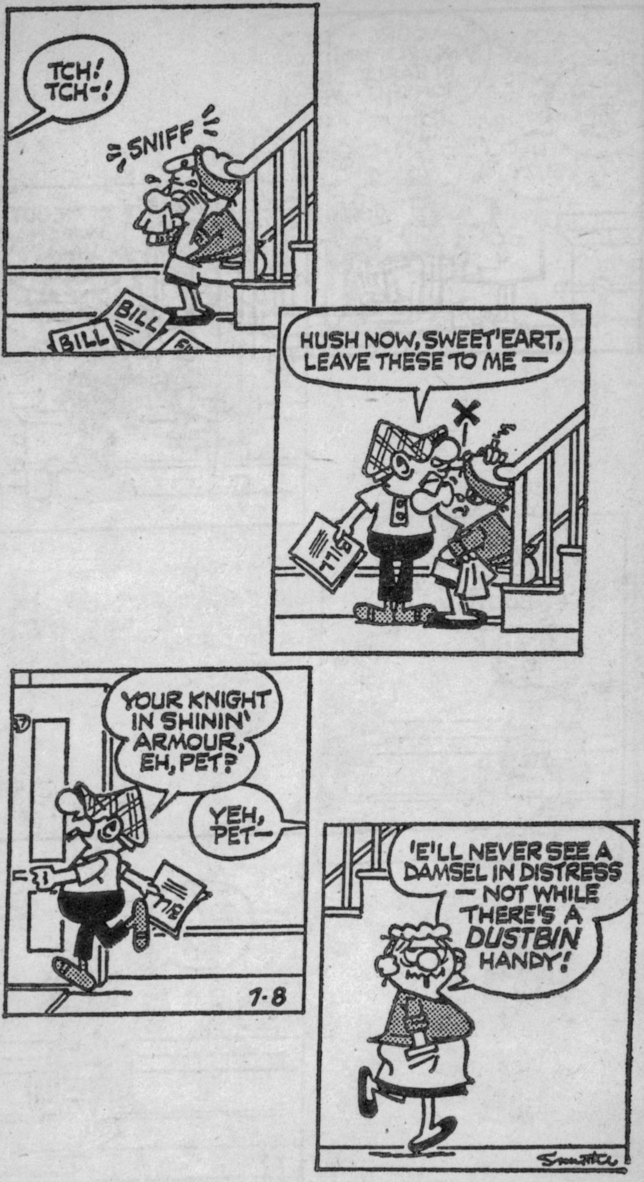
TCH! TCH-!
SNIFF
BILL
BILL
HUSH NOW, SWEET'EART, LEAVE THESE TO ME —
BILL
YOUR KNIGHT IN SHININ' ARMOUR, EH, PET?
YEH, PET—
BILL
7-8
'E'LL NEVER SEE A DAMSEL IN DISTRESS — NOT WHILE THERE'S A DUSTBIN HANDY!
Smythe

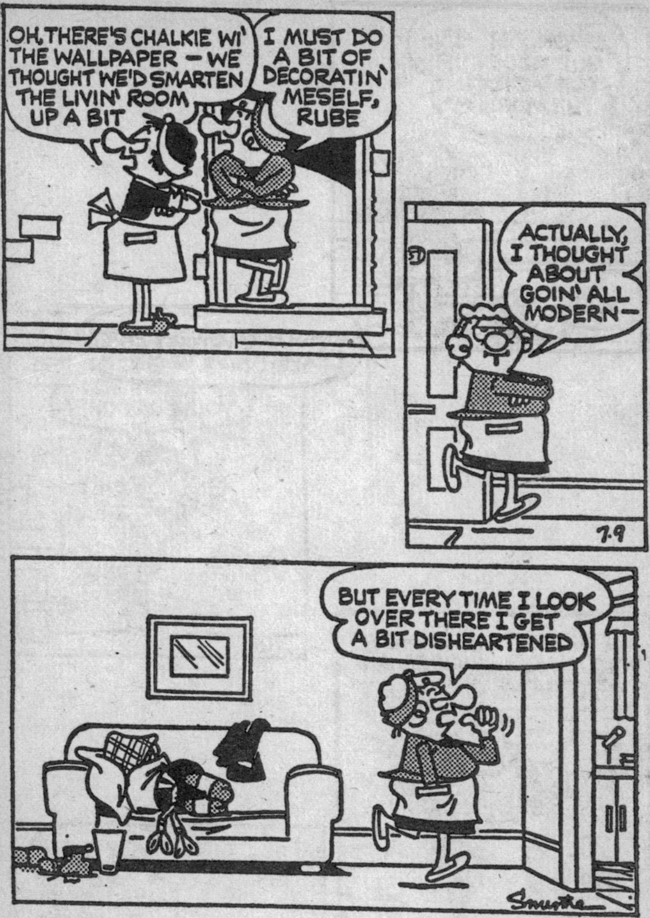
OH, THERE'S CHALKIE WI' THE WALLPAPER — WE THOUGHT WE'D SMARTEN THE LIVIN' ROOM UP A BIT
I MUST DO A BIT OF DECORATIN' MESELF, RUBE
ACTUALLY, I THOUGHT ABOUT GOIN' ALL MODERN—
7·9
BUT EVERY TIME I LOOK OVER THERE I GET A BIT DISHEARTENED
Smythe

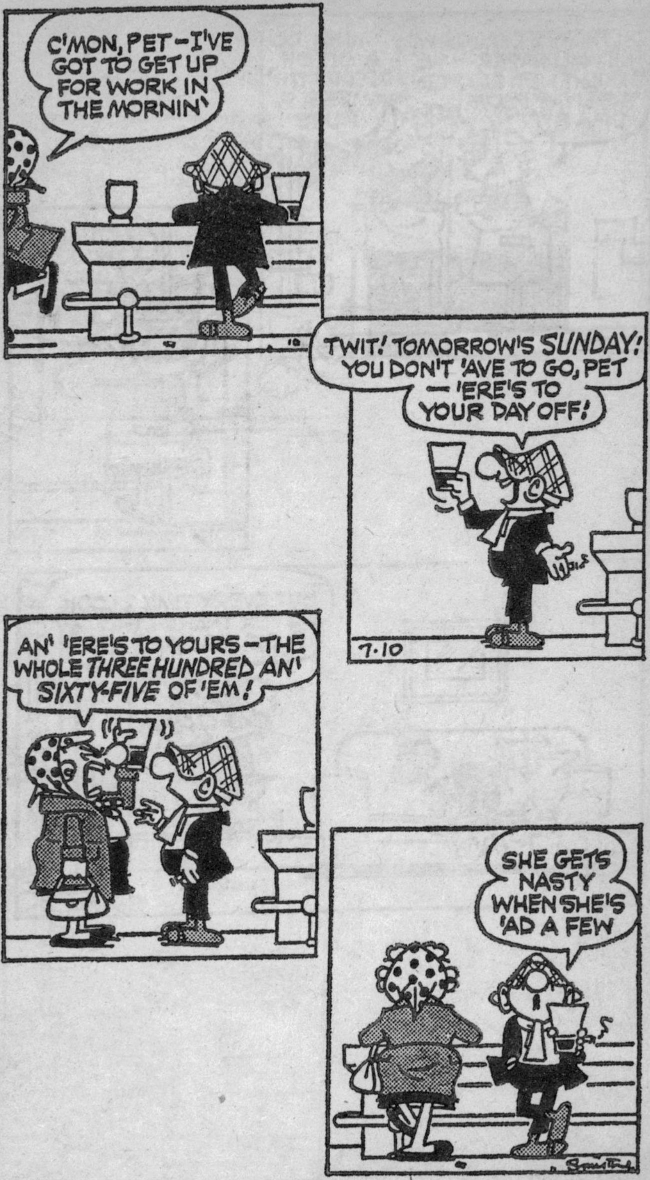
C'MON, PET—I'VE GOT TO GET UP FOR WORK IN THE MORNIN'
TWIT! TOMORROW'S *SUNDAY!* YOU DON'T 'AVE TO GO, PET — 'ERE'S TO YOUR DAY OFF!
7·10
AN' 'ERE'S TO YOURS—THE WHOLE *THREE HUNDRED AN' SIXTY-FIVE* OF 'EM!
SHE GETS NASTY WHEN SHE'S 'AD A FEW

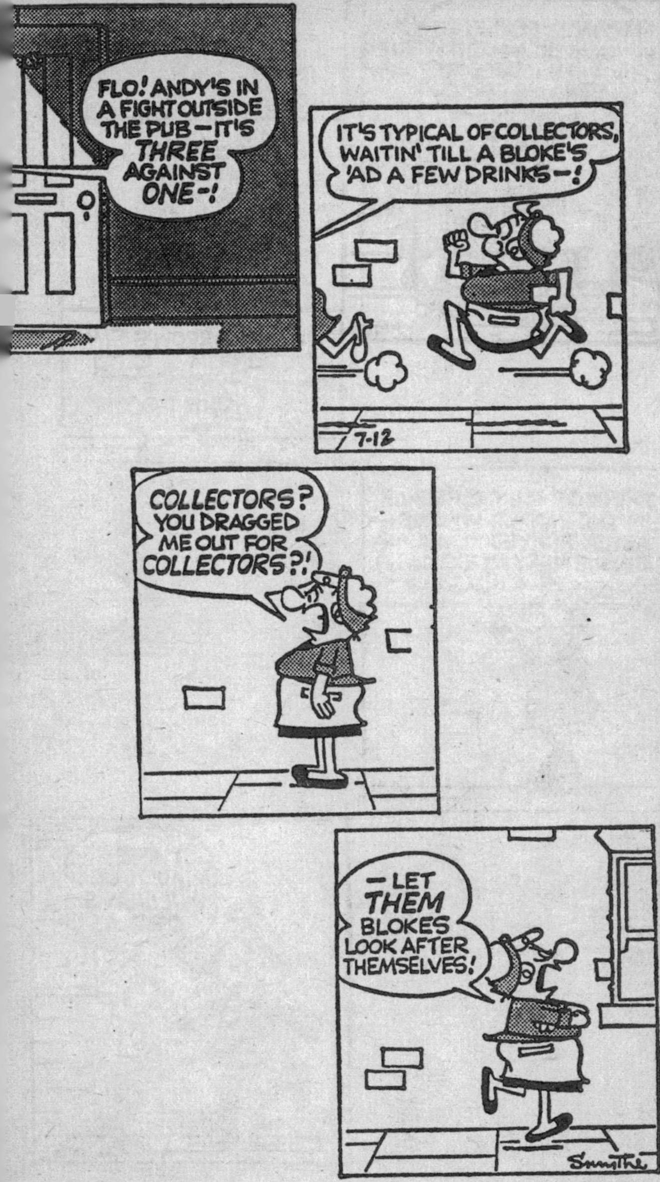

FLO! ANDY'S IN A FIGHT OUTSIDE THE PUB—IT'S THREE AGAINST ONE—!
IT'S TYPICAL OF COLLECTORS, WAITIN' TILL A BLOKE'S 'AD A FEW DRINKS—!
7-12
COLLECTORS? YOU DRAGGED ME OUT FOR COLLECTORS?!
—LET THEM BLOKES LOOK AFTER THEMSELVES!
Smythe

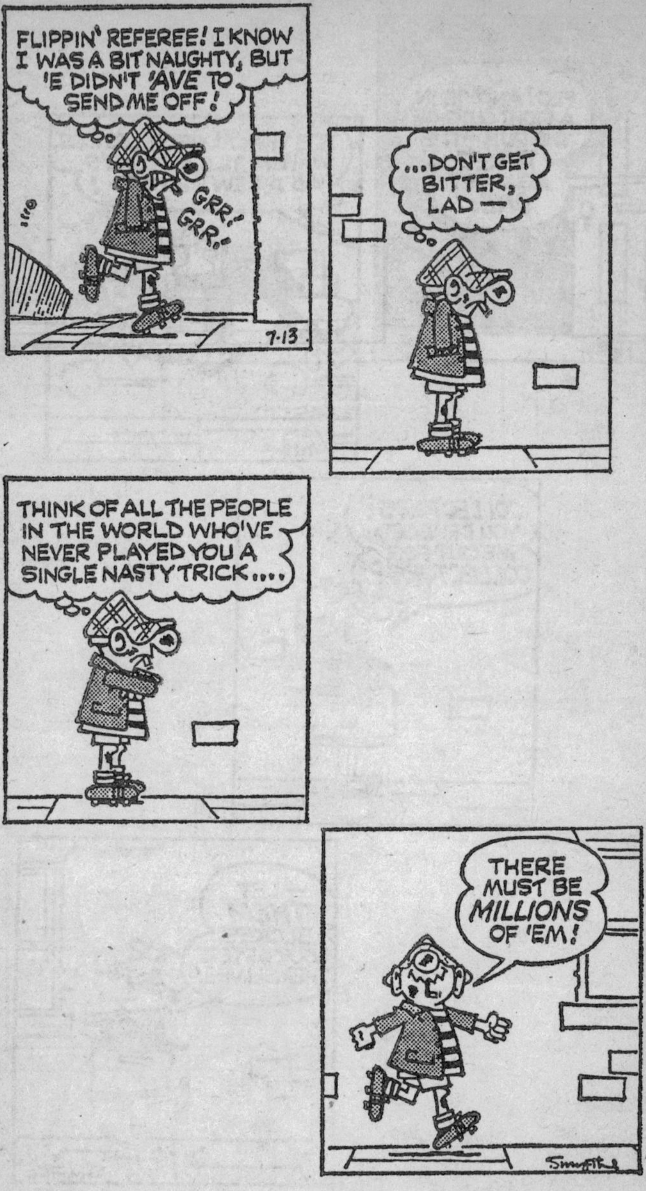
FLIPPIN' REFEREE! I KNOW I WAS A BIT NAUGHTY, BUT 'E DIDN'T 'AVE TO SEND ME OFF!
GRR! GRR!
7-13
...DON'T GET BITTER, LAD —
THINK OF ALL THE PEOPLE IN THE WORLD WHO'VE NEVER PLAYED YOU A SINGLE NASTY TRICK....
THERE MUST BE MILLIONS OF 'EM!
Smythe

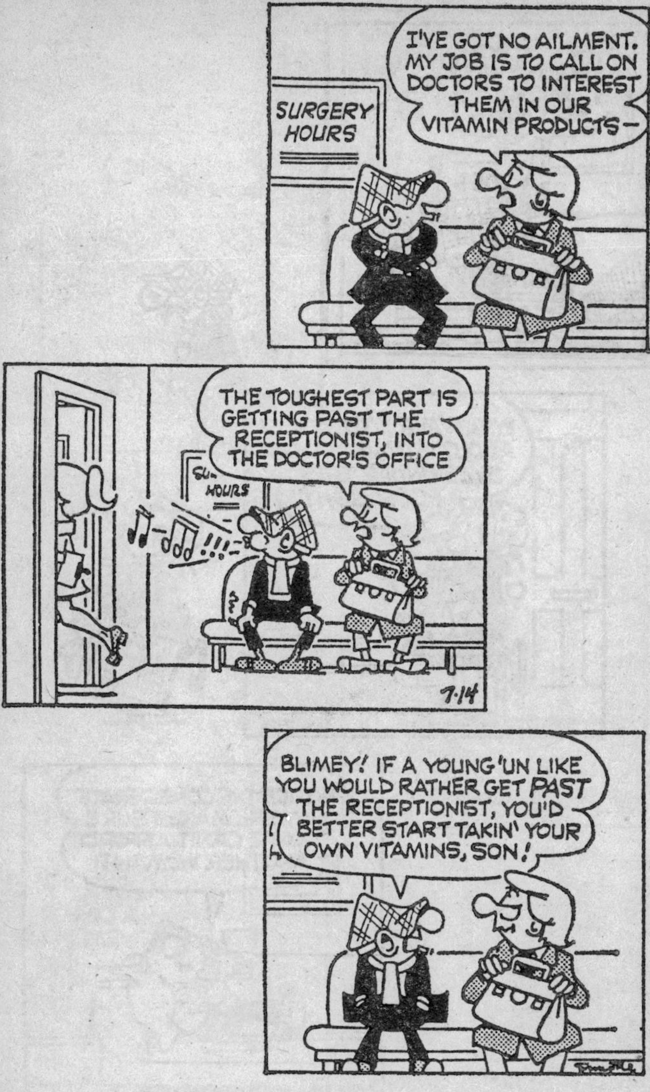
SURGERY HOURS
I'VE GOT NO AILMENT. MY JOB IS TO CALL ON DOCTORS TO INTEREST THEM IN OUR VITAMIN PRODUCTS—
THE TOUGHEST PART IS GETTING PAST THE RECEPTIONIST, INTO THE DOCTOR'S OFFICE
7·14
BLIMEY! IF A YOUNG 'UN LIKE YOU WOULD RATHER GET PAST THE RECEPTIONIST, YOU'D BETTER START TAKIN' YOUR OWN VITAMINS, SON!

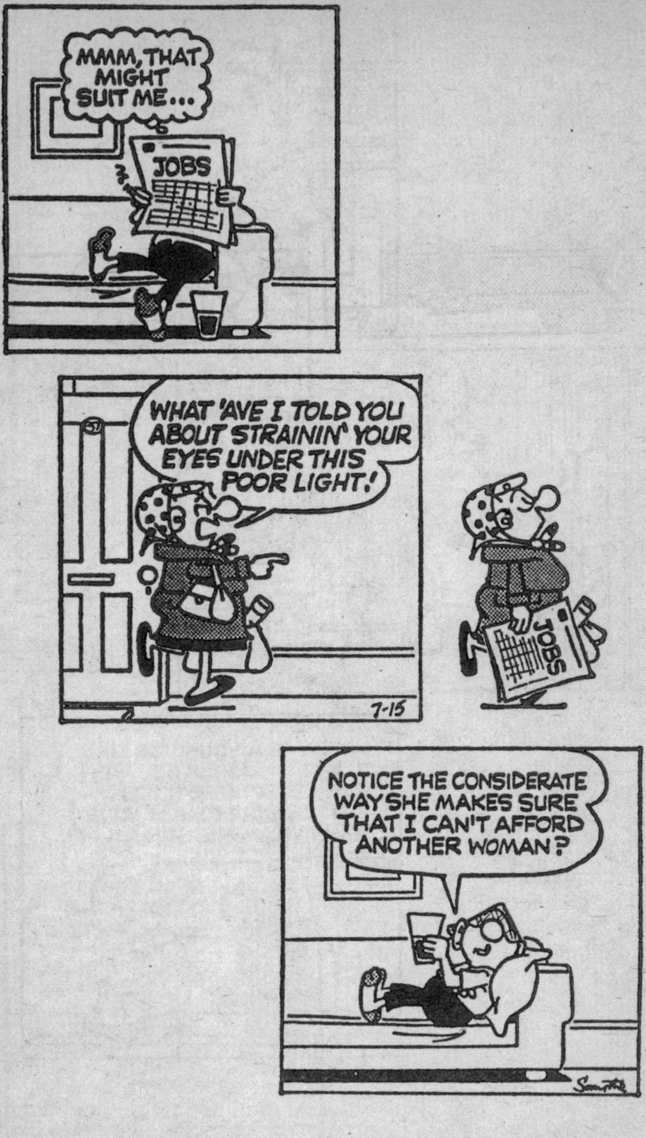
MMM, THAT MIGHT SUIT ME...
JOBS
WHAT 'AVE I TOLD YOU ABOUT STRAININ' YOUR EYES UNDER THIS POOR LIGHT!
7-15
JOBS
NOTICE THE CONSIDERATE WAY SHE MAKES SURE THAT I CAN'T AFFORD ANOTHER WOMAN?

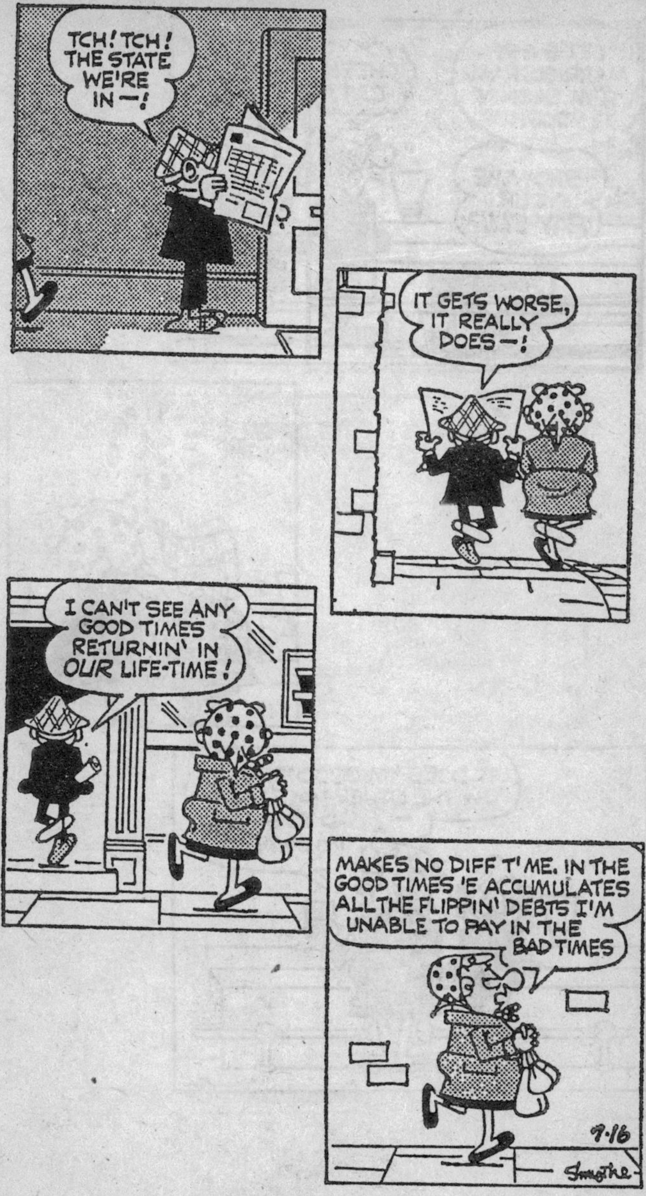
TCH! TCH! THE STATE WE'RE IN—!
IT GETS WORSE, IT REALLY DOES—!
I CAN'T SEE ANY GOOD TIMES RETURNIN' IN *OUR* LIFE-TIME!
MAKES NO DIFF T' ME. IN THE GOOD TIMES 'E ACCUMULATES ALL THE FLIPPIN' DEBTS I'M UNABLE TO PAY IN THE BAD TIMES
9·16
Smythe

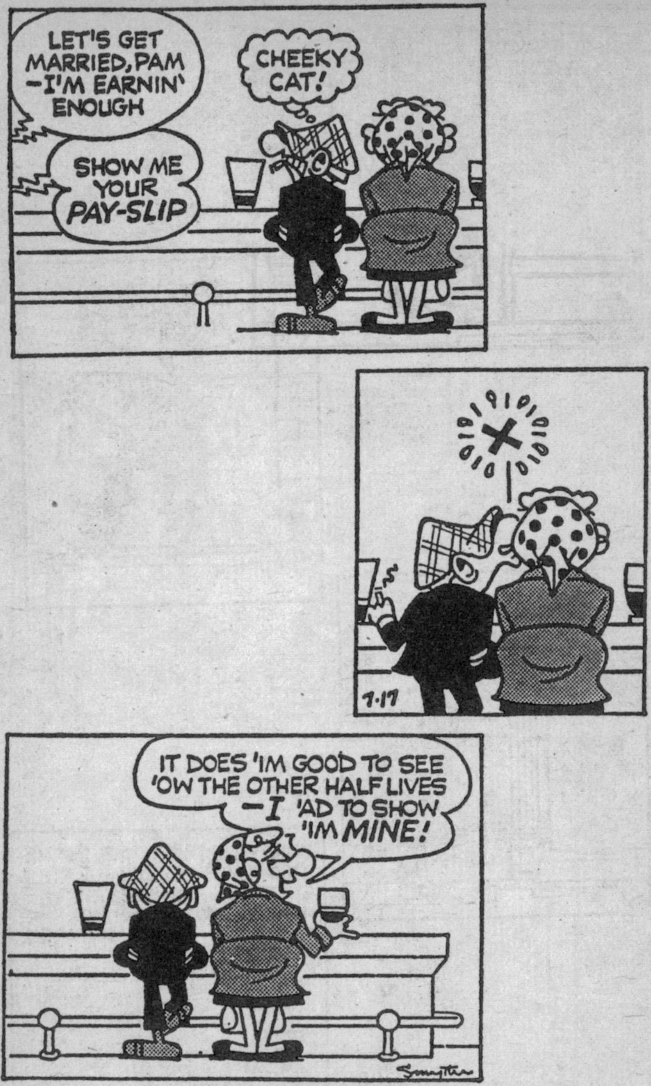
LET'S GET MARRIED, PAM –I'M EARNIN' ENOUGH
CHEEKY CAT!
SHOW ME YOUR PAY-SLIP
7·17
IT DOES 'IM GOOD TO SEE 'OW THE OTHER HALF LIVES –I 'AD TO SHOW 'IM MINE!
Smythe

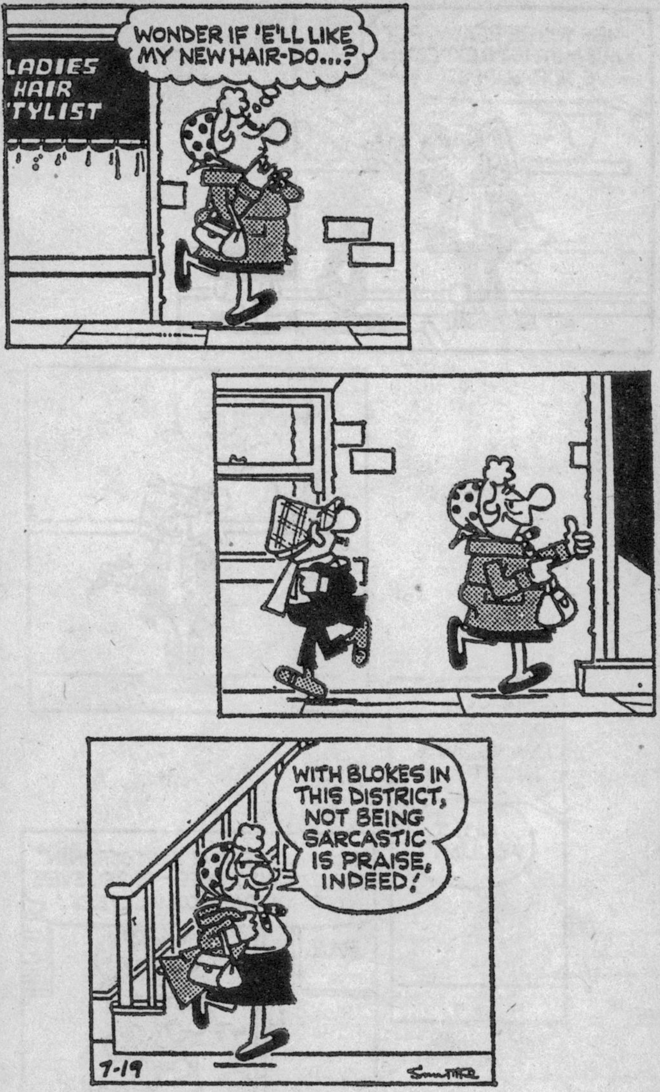
LADIES
HAIR
'TYLIST
WONDER IF 'E'LL LIKE MY NEW HAIR-DO...?
WITH BLOKES IN THIS DISTRICT, NOT BEING SARCASTIC IS PRAISE, INDEED!
7-19

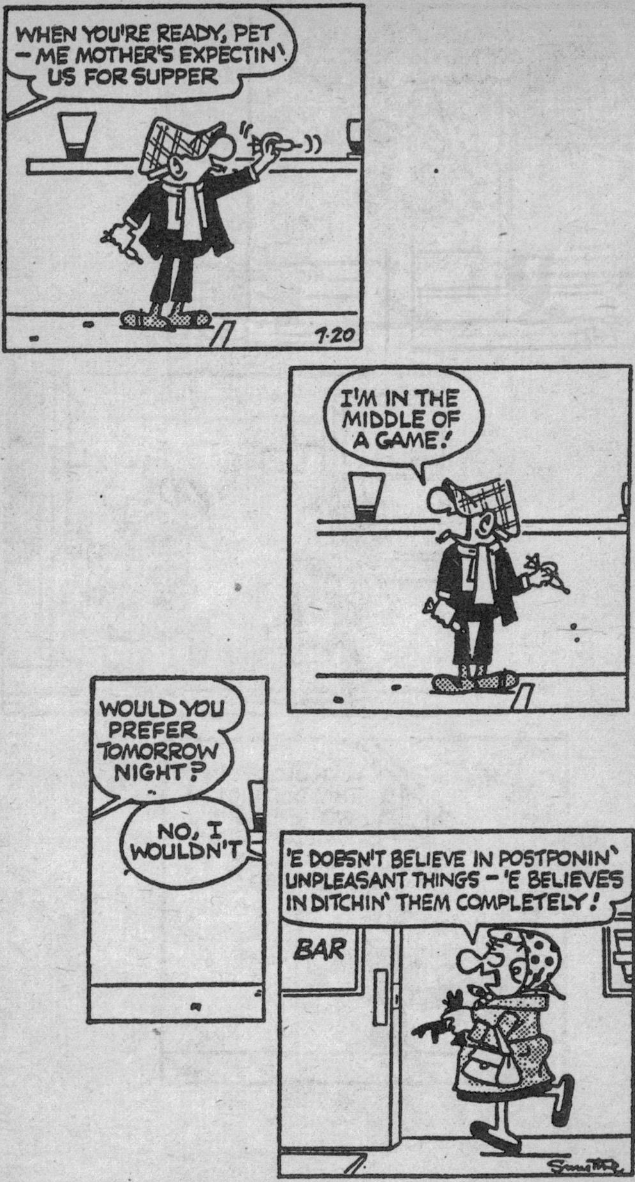

WHEN YOU'RE READY, PET – ME MOTHER'S EXPECTIN' US FOR SUPPER
7·20
I'M IN THE MIDDLE OF A GAME!
WOULD YOU PREFER TOMORROW NIGHT?
NO, I WOULDN'T
'E DOESN'T BELIEVE IN POSTPONIN' UNPLEASANT THINGS – 'E BELIEVES IN DITCHIN' THEM COMPLETELY!
BAR

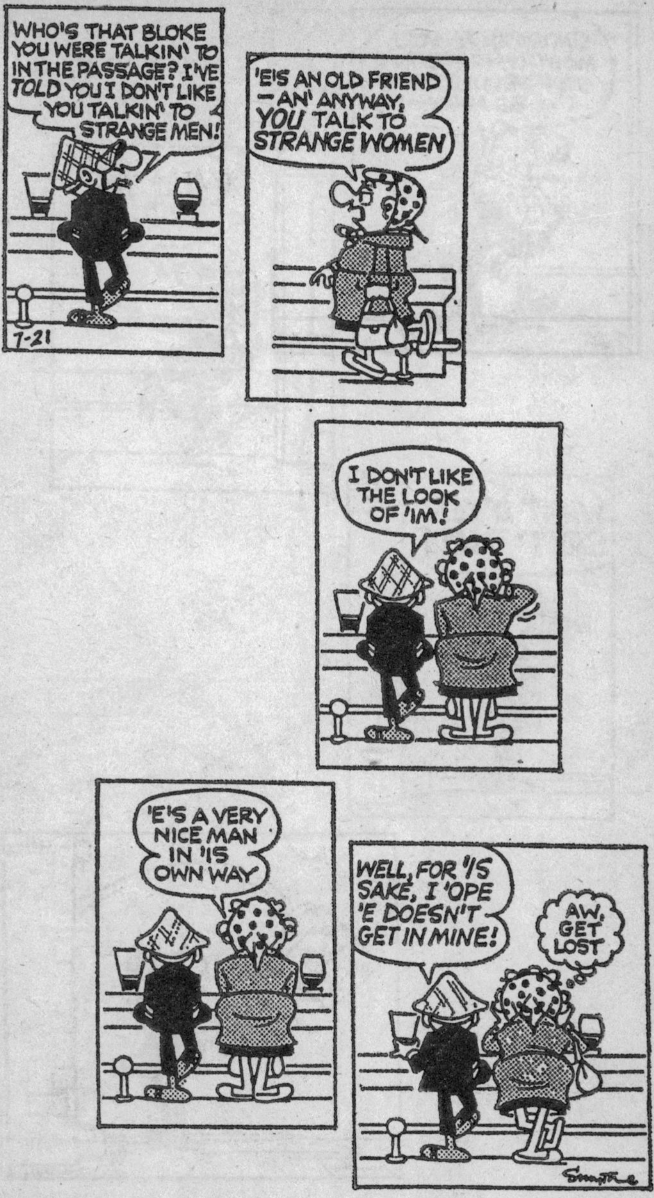
WHO'S THAT BLOKE YOU WERE TALKIN' TO IN THE PASSAGE? I'VE TOLD YOU I DON'T LIKE YOU TALKIN' TO STRANGE MEN!
7-21
'E'S AN OLD FRIEND —AN' ANYWAY, YOU TALK TO STRANGE WOMEN
I DON'T LIKE THE LOOK OF 'IM!
'E'S A VERY NICE MAN IN 'IS OWN WAY
WELL, FOR 'IS SAKE, I 'OPE 'E DOESN'T GET IN MINE!
AW, GET LOST
Smythe

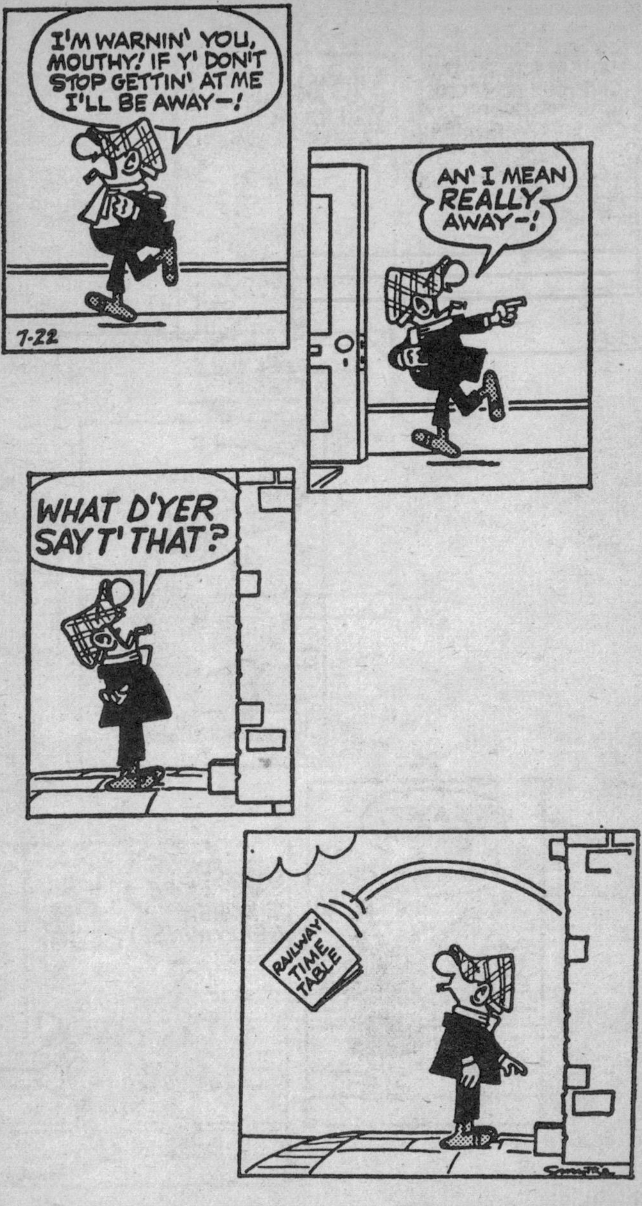
I'M WARNIN' YOU, MOUTHY! IF Y' DON'T STOP GETTIN' AT ME I'LL BE AWAY—!
7-22
AN' I MEAN REALLY AWAY—!
WHAT D'YER SAY T' THAT?
RAILWAY TIME TABLE

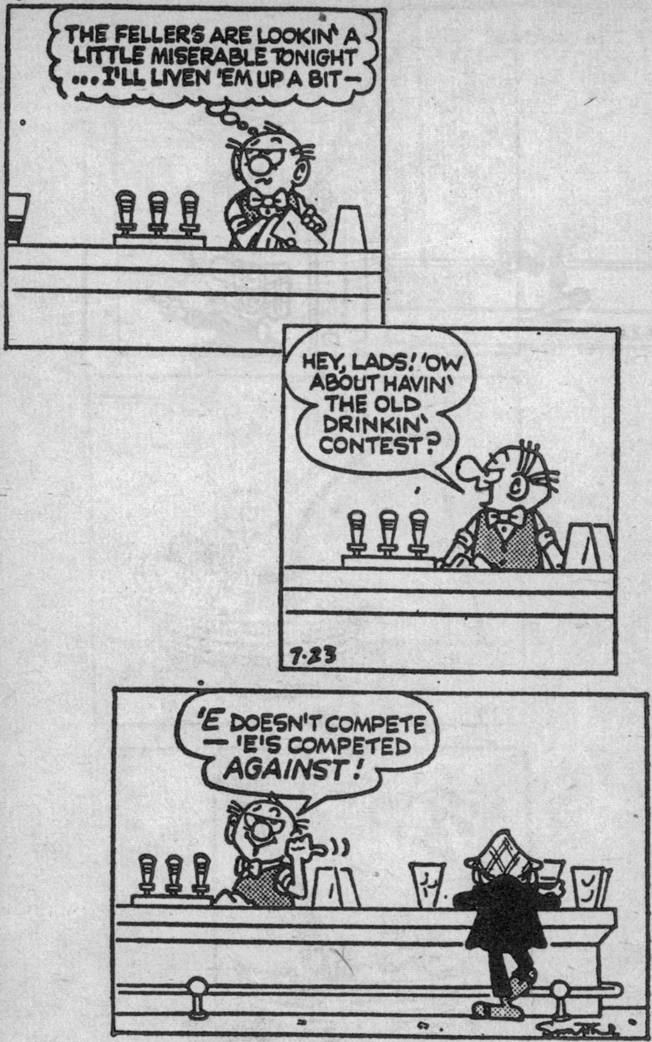
THE FELLERS ARE LOOKIN' A LITTLE MISERABLE TONIGHT ... I'LL LIVEN 'EM UP A BIT—
HEY, LADS! 'OW ABOUT HAVIN' THE OLD DRINKIN' CONTEST?
7·23
'E DOESN'T COMPETE — 'E'S COMPETED AGAINST!

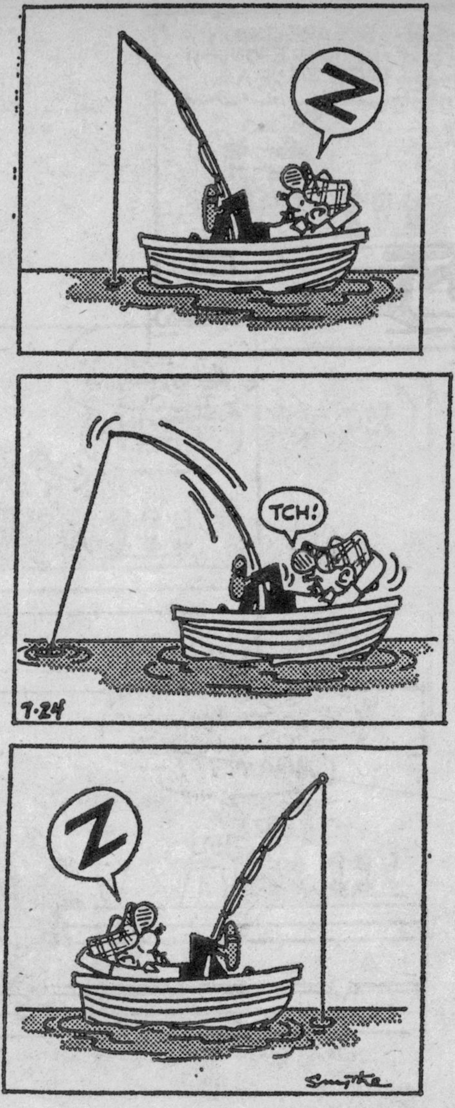
Z
TCH!
7·24
Z
Smythe

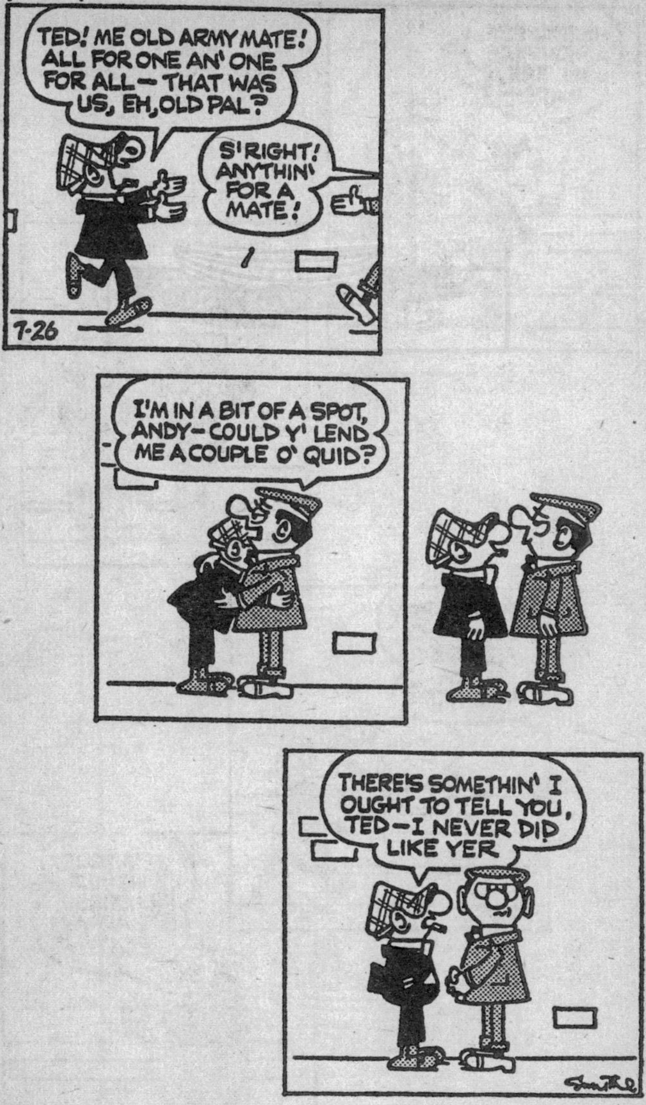
TED! ME OLD ARMY MATE! ALL FOR ONE AN' ONE FOR ALL — THAT WAS US, EH, OLD PAL?
S'RIGHT! ANYTHIN' FOR A MATE!
7-26
I'M IN A BIT OF A SPOT, ANDY — COULD Y' LEND ME A COUPLE O' QUID?
THERE'S SOMETHIN' I OUGHT TO TELL YOU, TED — I NEVER DID LIKE YER

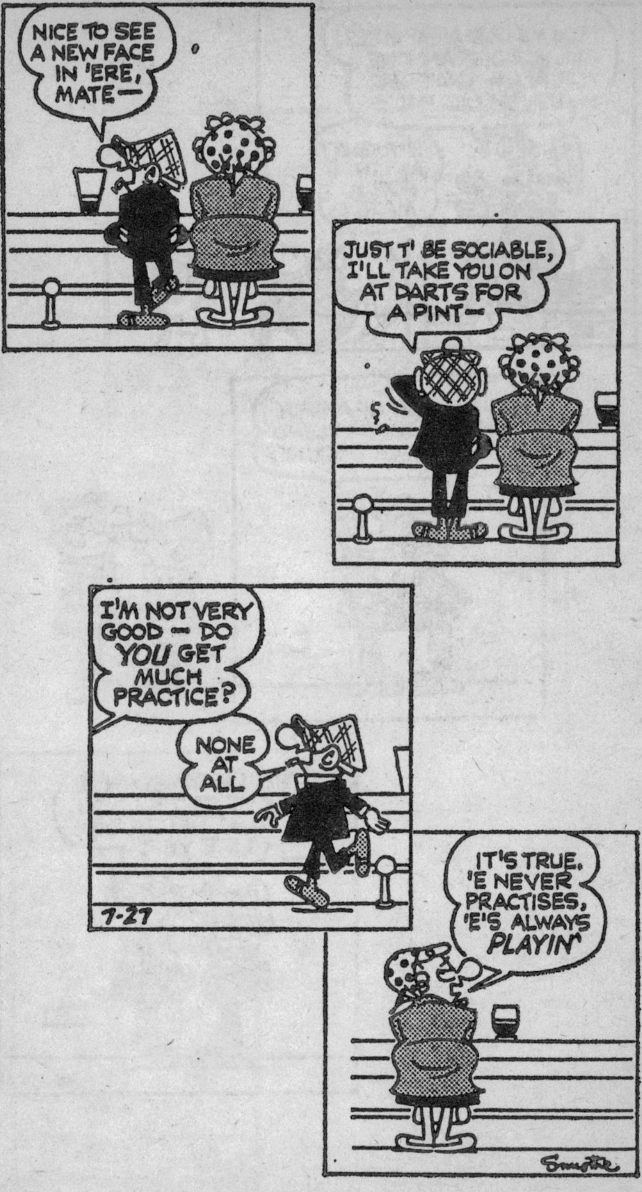
NICE TO SEE A NEW FACE IN 'ERE, MATE—
JUST T' BE SOCIABLE, I'LL TAKE YOU ON AT DARTS FOR A PINT—
I'M NOT VERY GOOD — DO *YOU* GET MUCH PRACTICE?
NONE AT ALL
7-27
IT'S TRUE. 'E NEVER PRACTISES, 'E'S ALWAYS *PLAYIN'*
Smythe

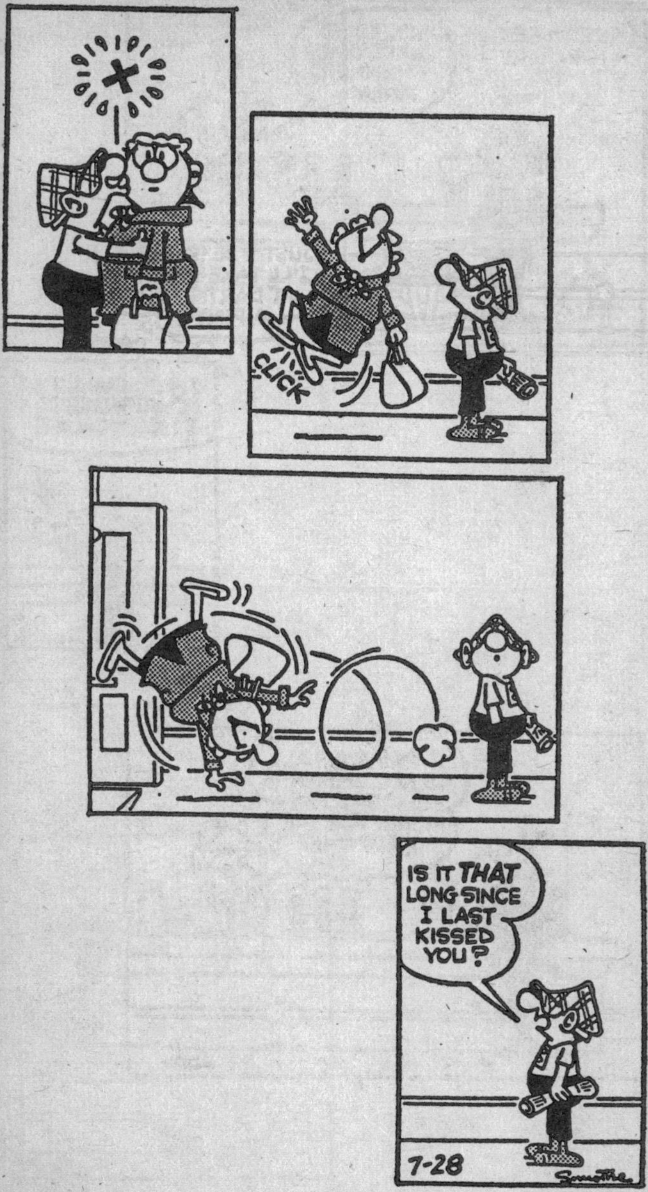
CLICK
IS IT THAT LONG SINCE I LAST KISSED YOU?
7-28
Smythe

YOU'LL BE LATE 'OME F' DINNER, ANDY—
7-29
THIS IS ALL THE NOURISHMENT I NEED, JACKIE
SIGH
IT PROVIDES ALL 'IS REQUIREMENTS — EXCEPT THE MONEY FOR THE NEXT ONE!
SMYTHE

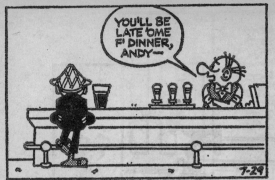

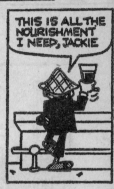

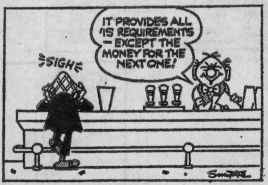

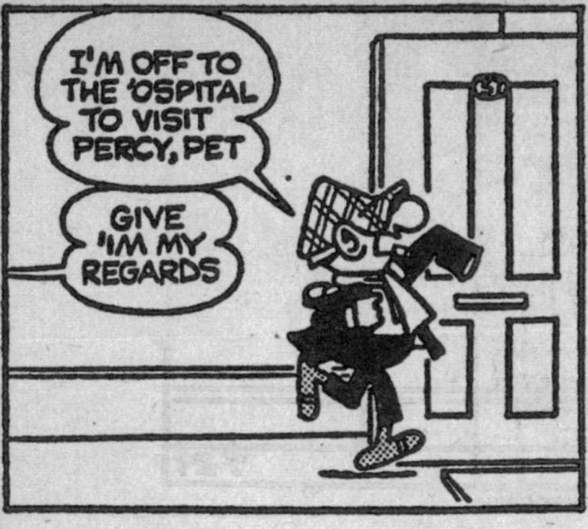
I'M OFF TO THE 'OSPITAL TO VISIT PERCY, PET
GIVE 'IM MY REGARDS

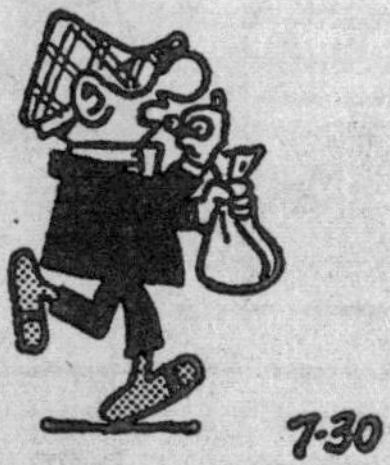
7-30

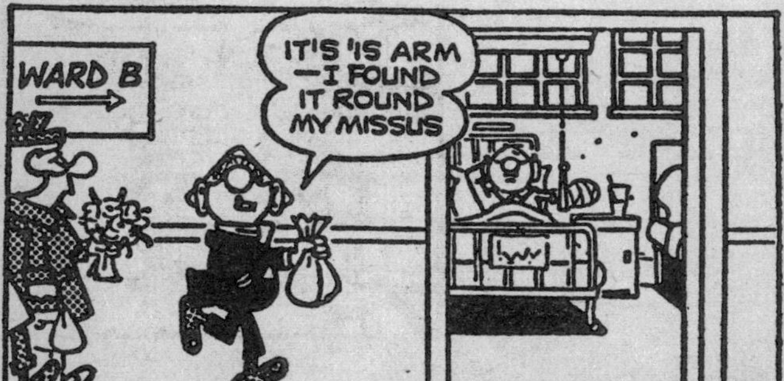
WARD B
IT'S 'IS ARM —I FOUND IT ROUND MY MISSUS
Smythe

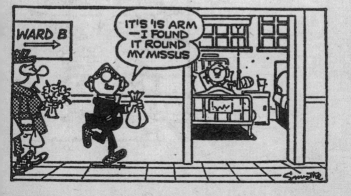

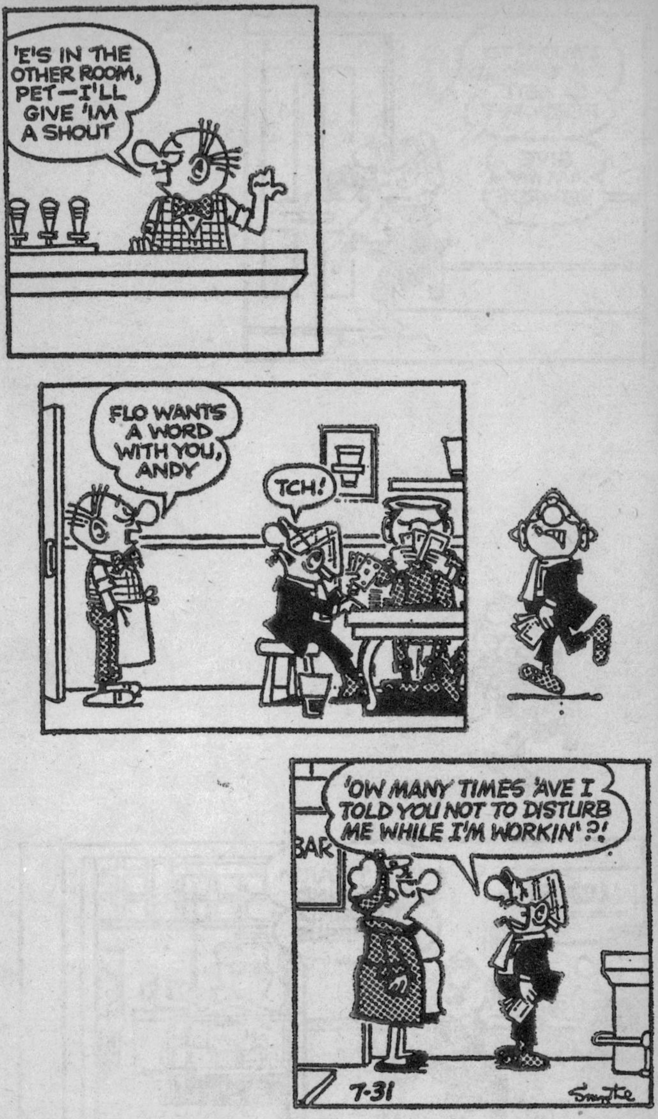
'E'S IN THE OTHER ROOM, PET—I'LL GIVE 'IM A SHOUT
FLO WANTS A WORD WITH YOU, ANDY
TCH!
'OW MANY TIMES 'AVE I TOLD YOU NOT TO DISTURB ME WHILE I'M WORKIN' ?!
BAR
7-31
Smythe

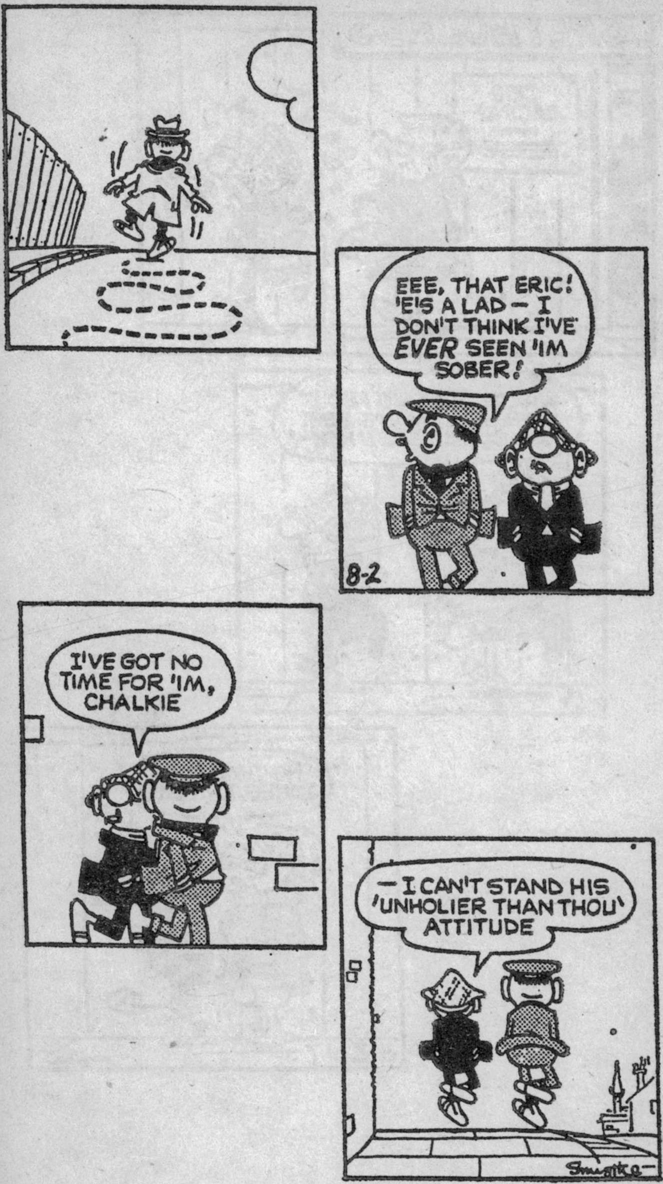
EEE, THAT ERIC! 'E'S A LAD — I DON'T THINK I'VE EVER SEEN 'IM SOBER!
8-2
I'VE GOT NO TIME FOR 'IM, CHALKIE
— I CAN'T STAND HIS 'UNHOLIER THAN THOU' ATTITUDE

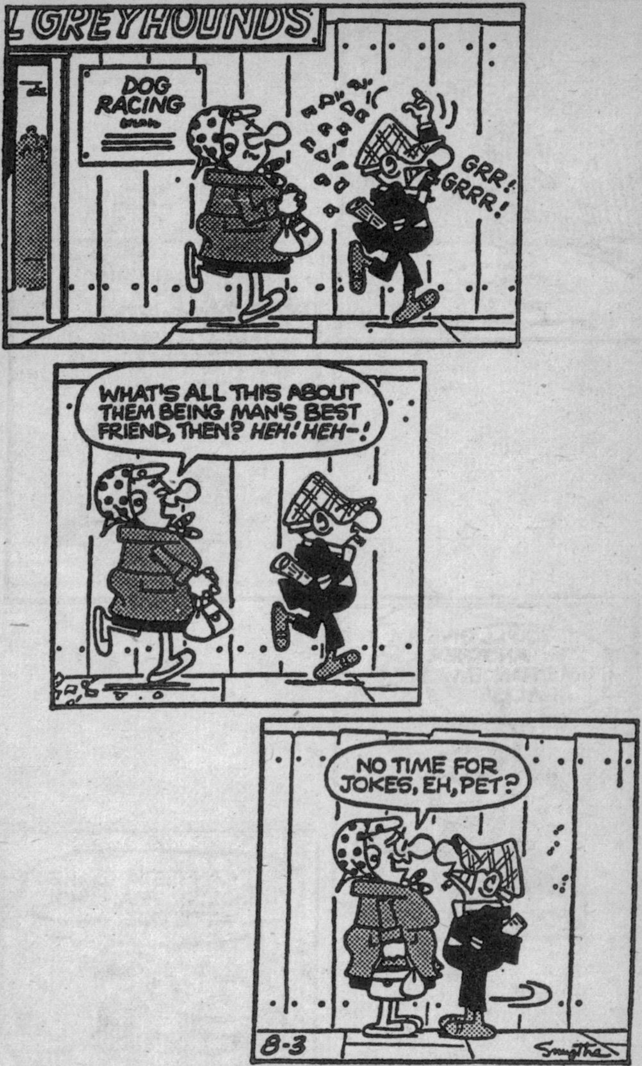
GREYHOUNDS
DOG RACING
GRR! GRRR!
WHAT'S ALL THIS ABOUT THEM BEING MAN'S BEST FRIEND, THEN? HEH! HEH-!
NO TIME FOR JOKES, EH, PET?
8-3
Smythe

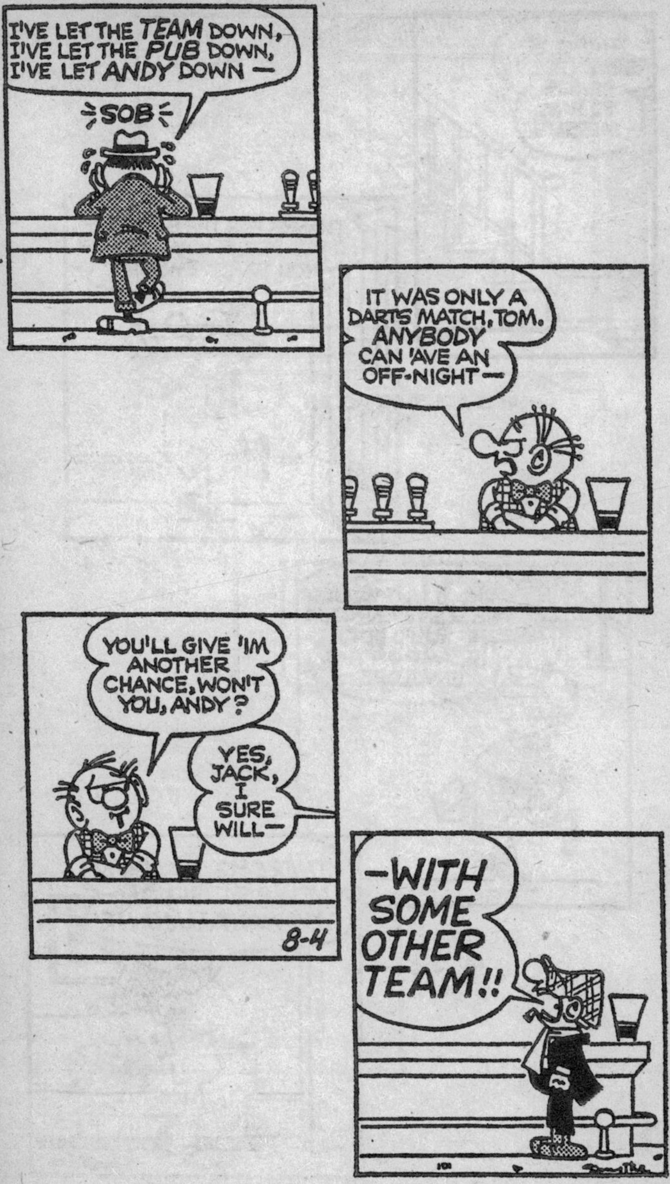
I'VE LET THE TEAM DOWN, I'VE LET THE PUB DOWN, I'VE LET ANDY DOWN —
SOB
IT WAS ONLY A DART'S MATCH, TOM. ANYBODY CAN 'AVE AN OFF-NIGHT —
YOU'LL GIVE 'IM ANOTHER CHANCE, WON'T YOU, ANDY?
YES, JACK, I SURE WILL—
8-4
—WITH SOME OTHER TEAM!!

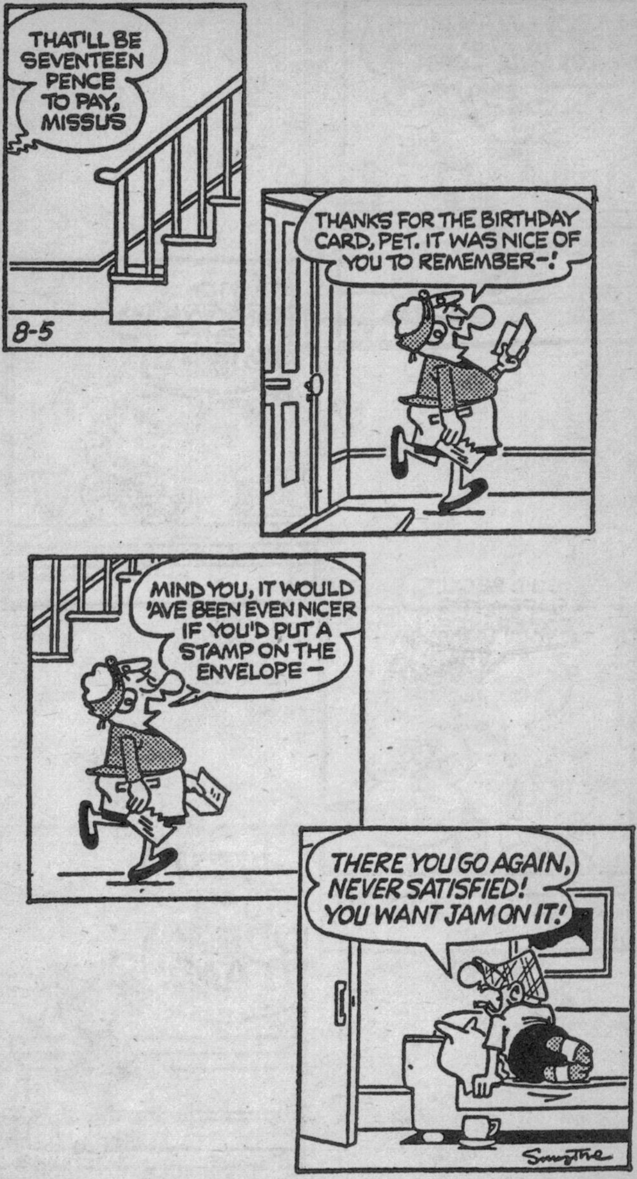
THAT'LL BE SEVENTEEN PENCE TO PAY, MISSUS
8-5
THANKS FOR THE BIRTHDAY CARD, PET. IT WAS NICE OF YOU TO REMEMBER–!
MIND YOU, IT WOULD 'AVE BEEN EVEN NICER IF YOU'D PUT A STAMP ON THE ENVELOPE –
THERE YOU GO AGAIN, NEVER SATISFIED! YOU WANT JAM ON IT!
Smythe

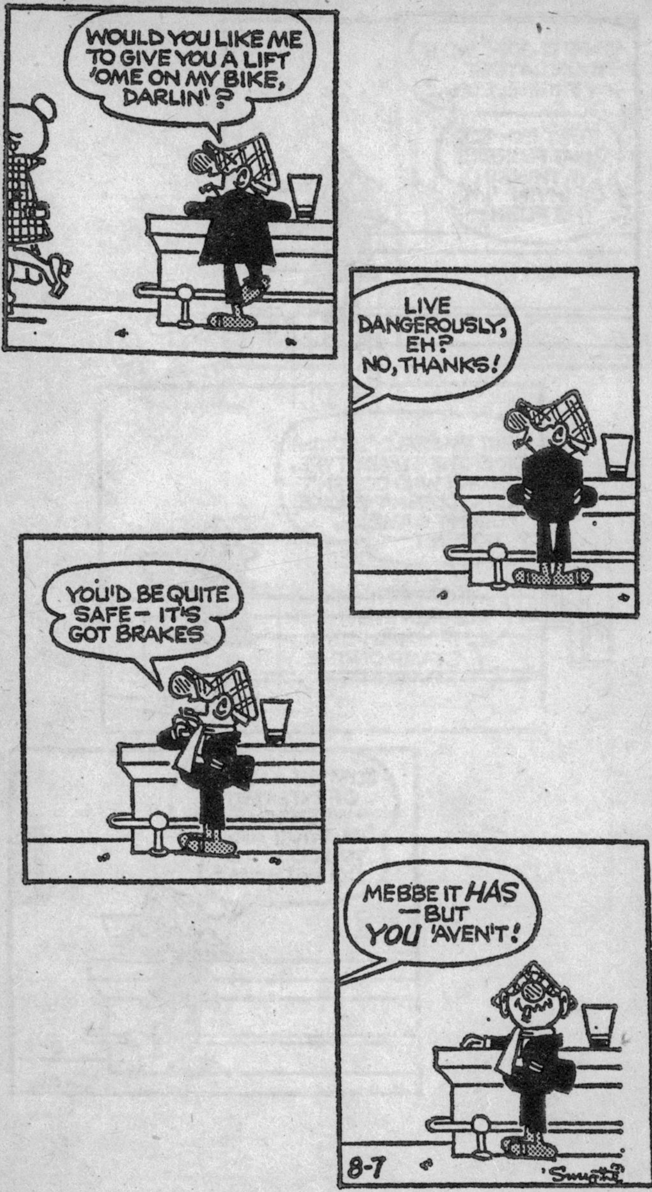
WOULD YOU LIKE ME TO GIVE YOU A LIFT 'OME ON MY BIKE, DARLIN'?
LIVE DANGEROUSLY, EH? NO, THANKS!
YOU'D BE QUITE SAFE – IT'S GOT BRAKES
MEBBE IT HAS — BUT YOU 'AVEN'T!
8-7
Smythe

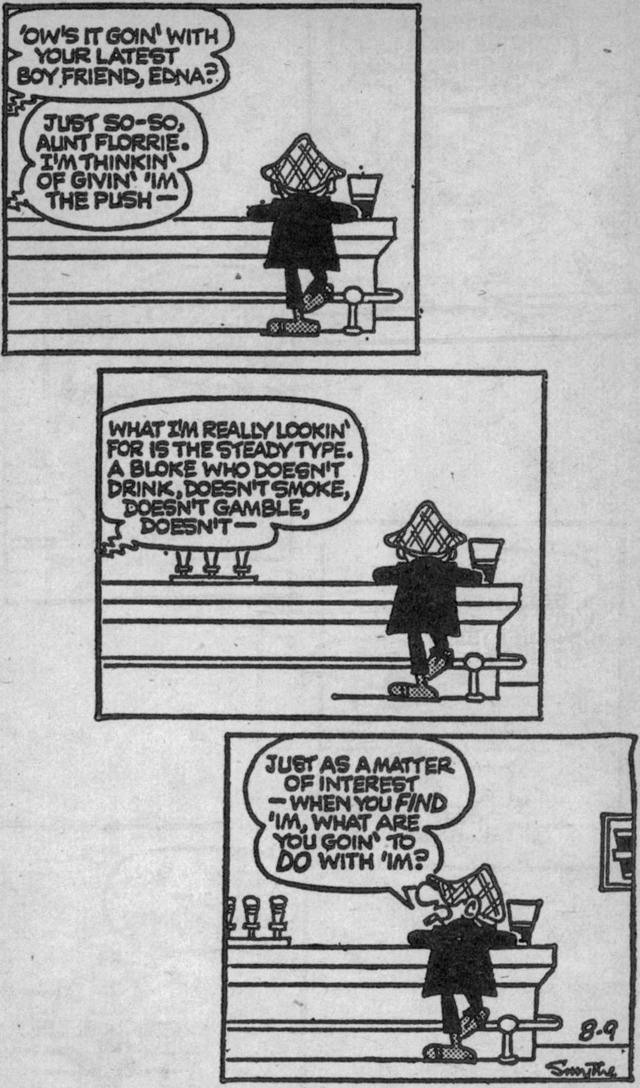
'OW'S IT GOIN' WITH YOUR LATEST BOY FRIEND, EDNA?
JUST SO-SO, AUNT FLORRIE. I'M THINKIN' OF GIVIN' 'IM THE PUSH —
WHAT I'M REALLY LOOKIN' FOR IS THE STEADY TYPE. A BLOKE WHO DOESN'T DRINK, DOESN'T SMOKE, DOESN'T GAMBLE, DOESN'T —
JUST AS A MATTER OF INTEREST — WHEN YOU FIND 'IM, WHAT ARE YOU GOIN' TO DO WITH 'IM?
8-9
Smythe

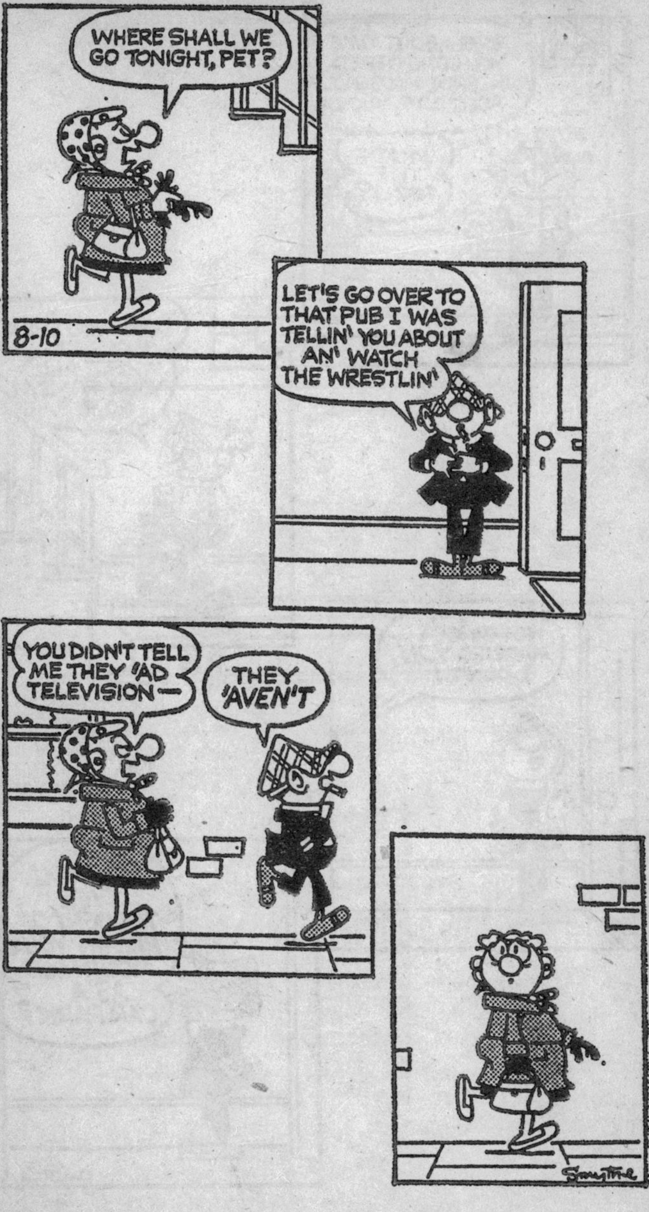
WHERE SHALL WE GO TONIGHT, PET?
8-10
LET'S GO OVER TO THAT PUB I WAS TELLIN' YOU ABOUT AN' WATCH THE WRESTLIN'
YOU DIDN'T TELL ME THEY 'AD TELEVISION—
THEY 'AVEN'T
Smythe

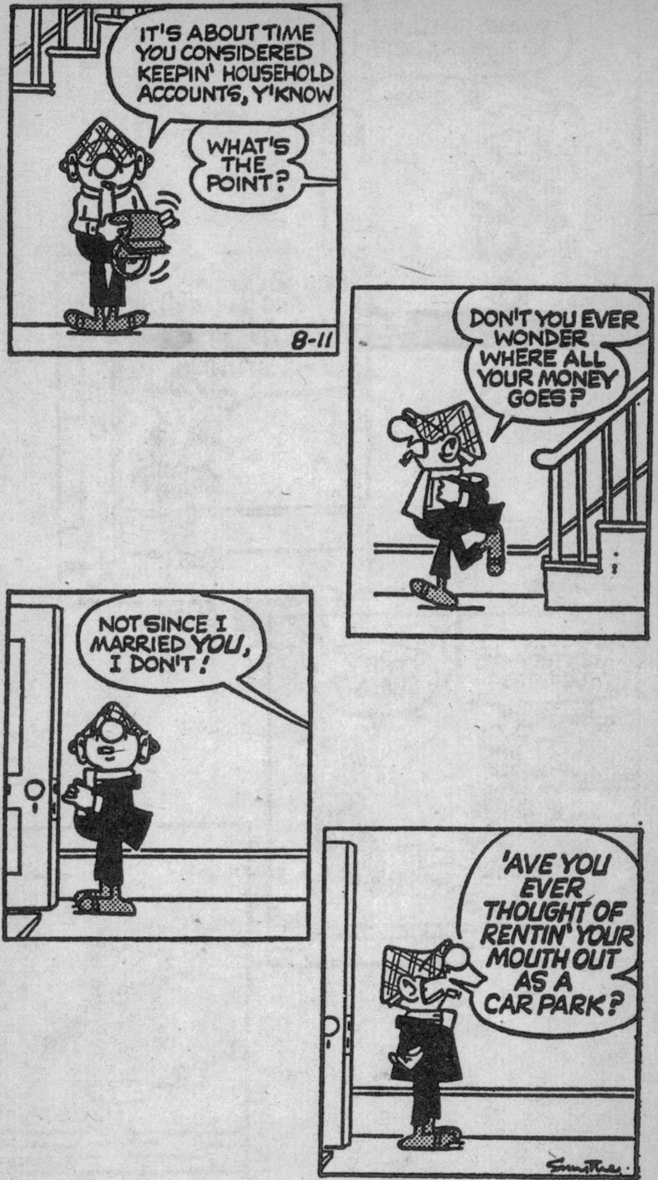
IT'S ABOUT TIME YOU CONSIDERED KEEPIN' HOUSEHOLD ACCOUNTS, Y'KNOW
WHAT'S THE POINT?
8-11
DON'T YOU EVER WONDER WHERE ALL YOUR MONEY GOES?
NOT SINCE I MARRIED YOU, I DON'T!
'AVE YOU EVER THOUGHT OF RENTIN' YOUR MOUTH OUT AS A CAR PARK?
Smythe

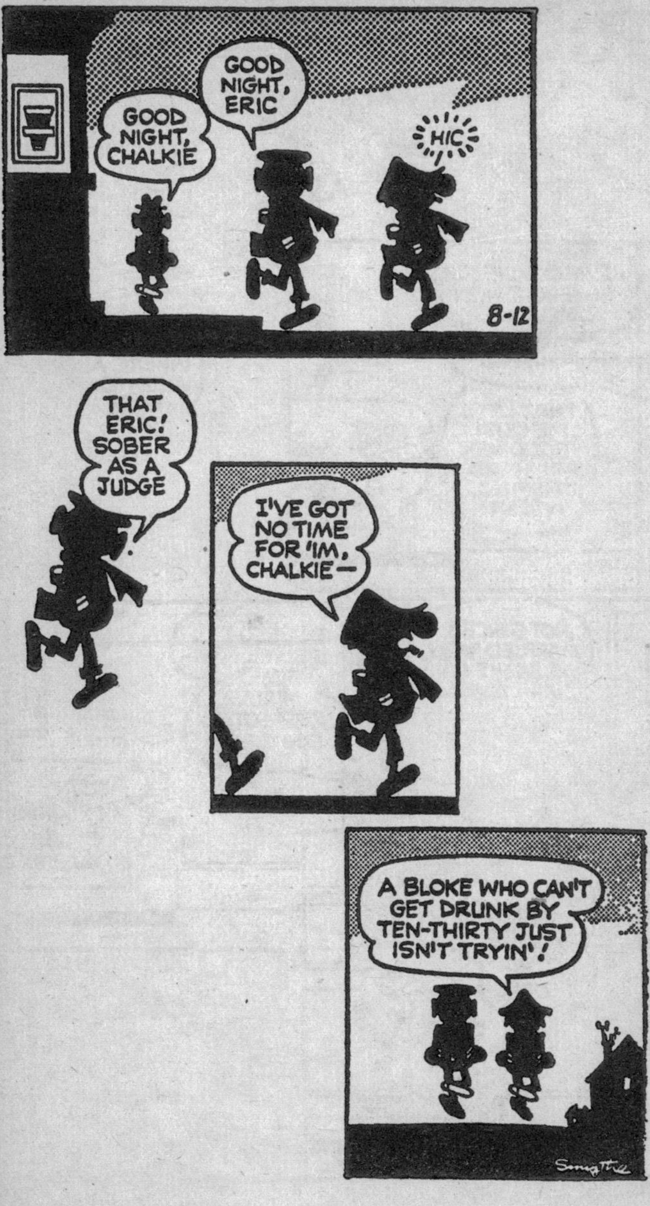
GOOD NIGHT, CHALKIE
GOOD NIGHT, ERIC
HIC
8-12
THAT ERIC! SOBER AS A JUDGE
I'VE GOT NO TIME FOR 'IM, CHALKIE—
A BLOKE WHO CAN'T GET DRUNK BY TEN-THIRTY JUST ISN'T TRYIN'!
Smythe

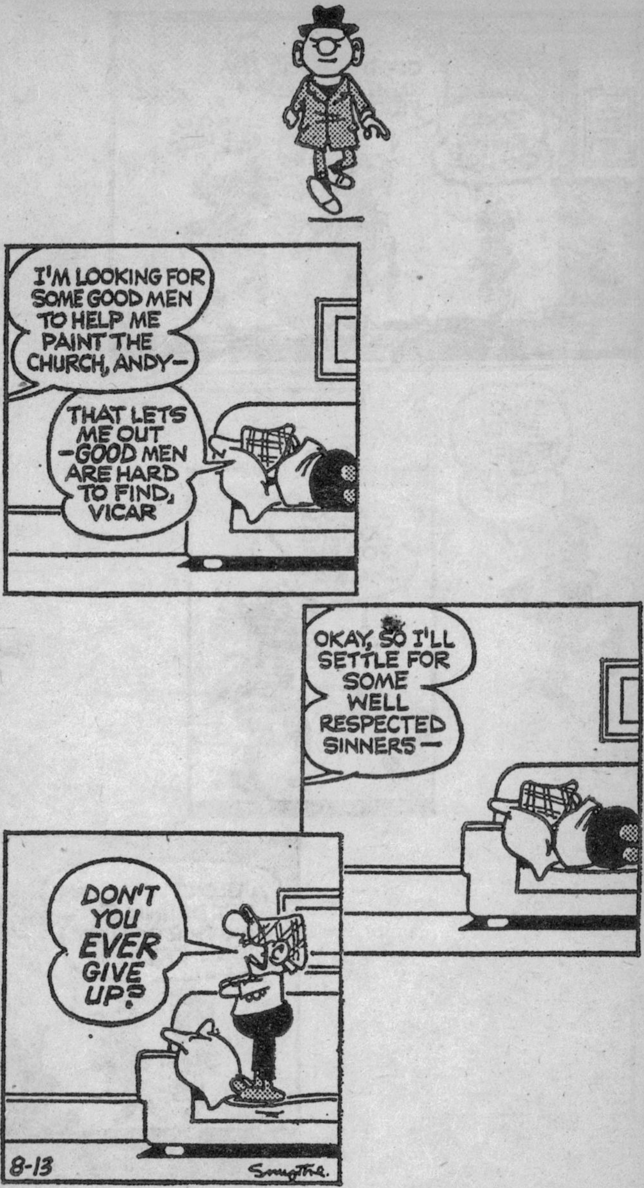
I'M LOOKING FOR SOME GOOD MEN TO HELP ME PAINT THE CHURCH, ANDY—
THAT LETS ME OUT —GOOD MEN ARE HARD TO FIND, VICAR
OKAY, SO I'LL SETTLE FOR SOME WELL RESPECTED SINNERS—
DON'T YOU EVER GIVE UP?
8-13
Smythe.

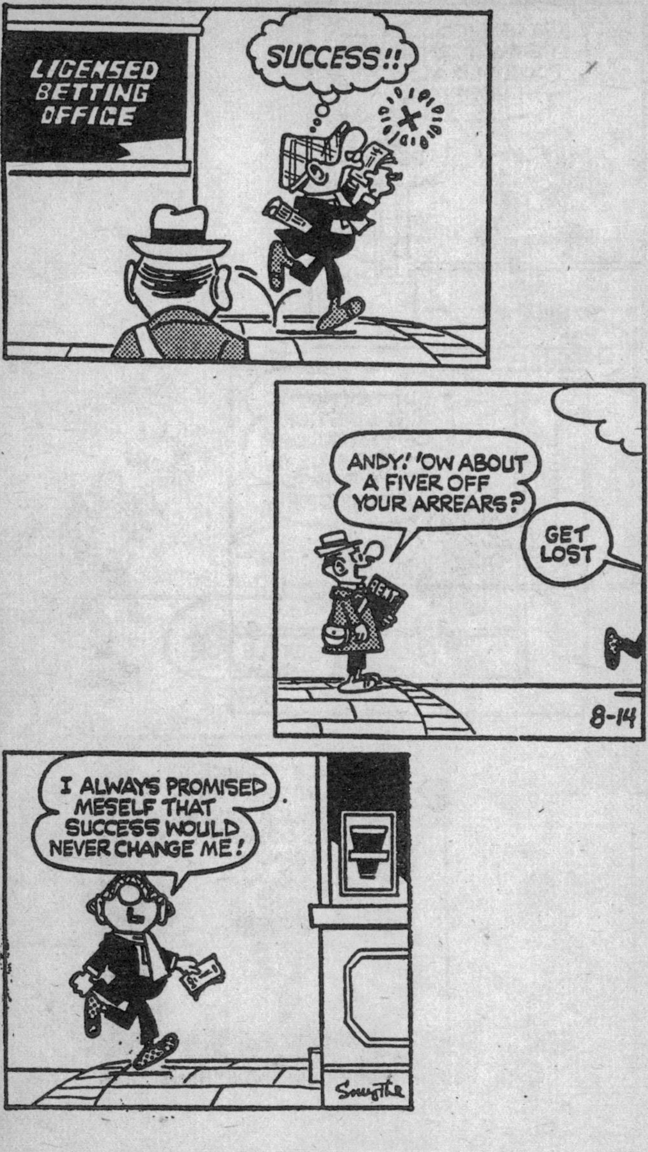
LICENSED BETTING OFFICE
SUCCESS!!
ANDY! 'OW ABOUT A FIVER OFF YOUR ARREARS?
GET LOST
RENT
8-14
I ALWAYS PROMISED MESELF THAT SUCCESS WOULD NEVER CHANGE ME!
Smythe

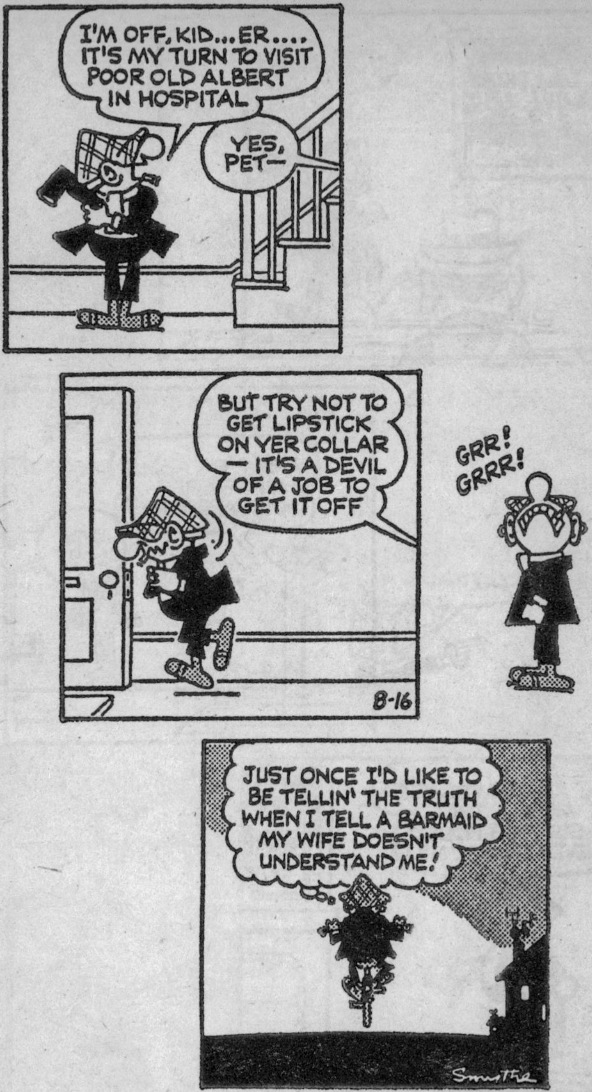
I'M OFF, KID... ER.... IT'S MY TURN TO VISIT POOR OLD ALBERT IN HOSPITAL
YES, PET—
BUT TRY NOT TO GET LIPSTICK ON YER COLLAR — IT'S A DEVIL OF A JOB TO GET IT OFF
8-16
GRR! GRRR!
JUST ONCE I'D LIKE TO BE TELLIN' THE TRUTH WHEN I TELL A BARMAID MY WIFE DOESN'T UNDERSTAND ME!
Smythe

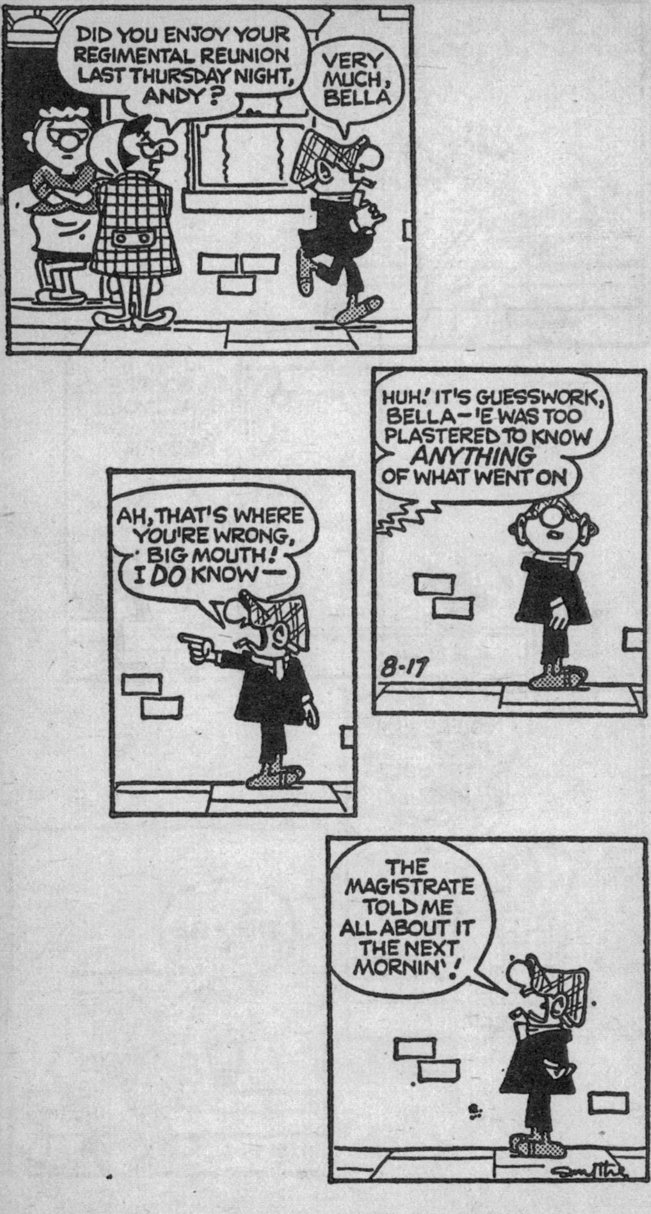
DID YOU ENJOY YOUR REGIMENTAL REUNION LAST THURSDAY NIGHT, ANDY?
VERY MUCH, BELLA
HUH! IT'S GUESSWORK, BELLA—'E WAS TOO PLASTERED TO KNOW *ANYTHING* OF WHAT WENT ON
8-17
AH, THAT'S WHERE YOU'RE WRONG, BIG MOUTH! I *DO* KNOW—
THE MAGISTRATE TOLD ME ALL ABOUT IT THE NEXT MORNIN'!
Smythe

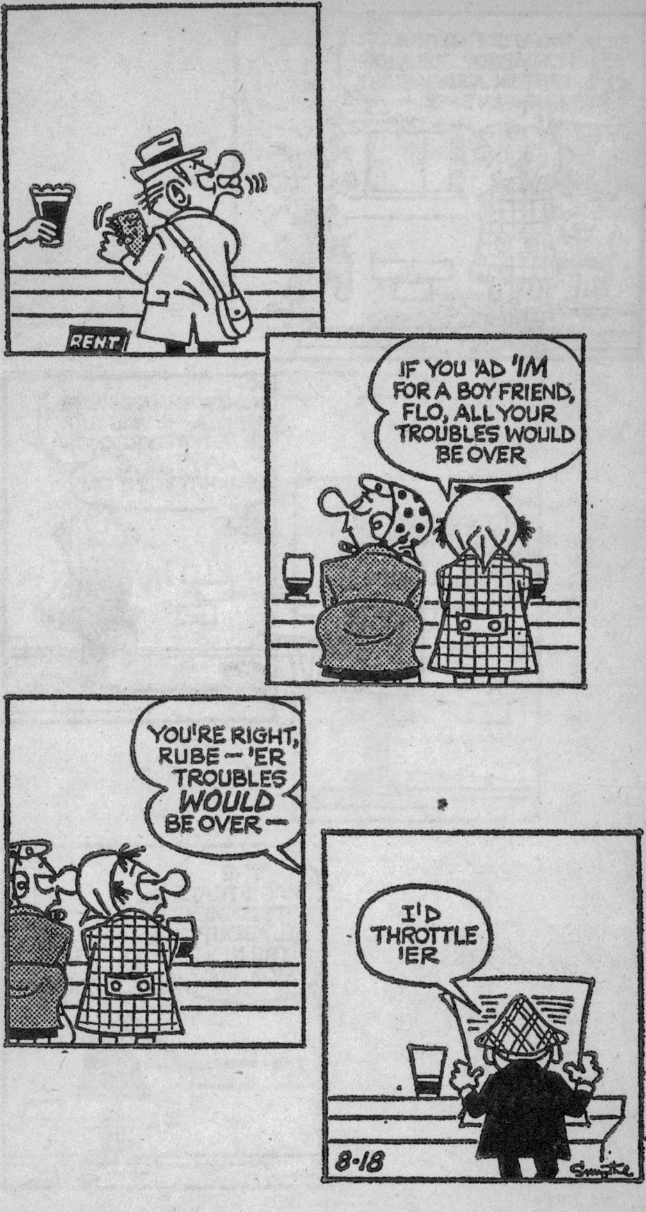
RENT
IF YOU 'AD 'IM FOR A BOY FRIEND, FLO, ALL YOUR TROUBLES WOULD BE OVER
YOU'RE RIGHT, RUBE — 'ER TROUBLES *WOULD* BE OVER —
I'D THROTTLE 'ER
8-18
Smythe

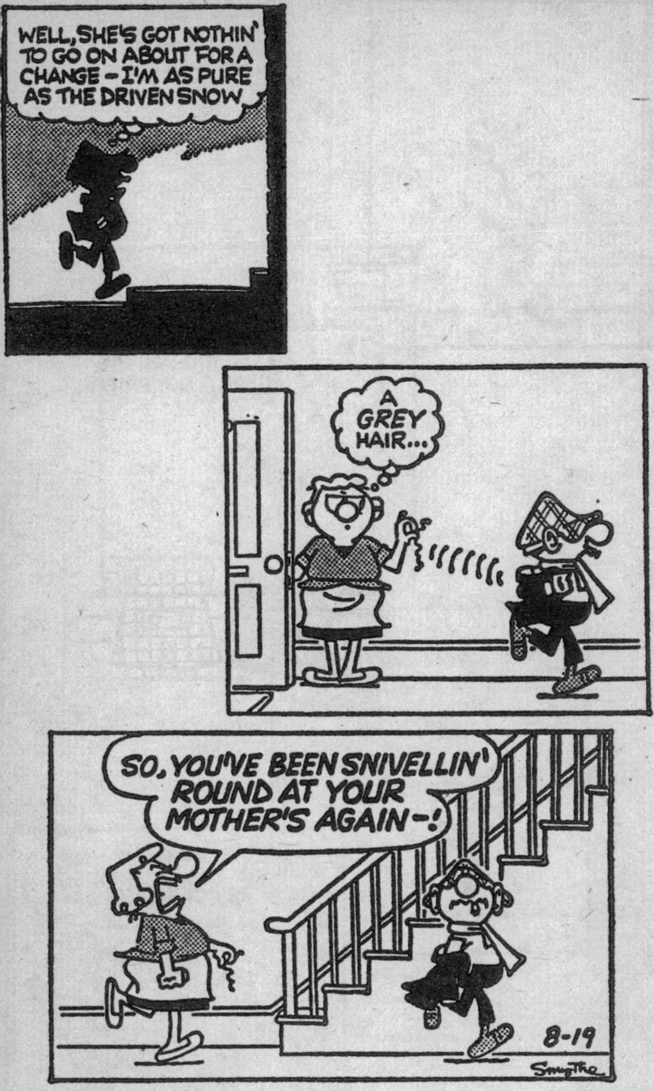
WELL, SHE'S GOT NOTHIN' TO GO ON ABOUT FOR A CHANGE – I'M AS PURE AS THE DRIVEN SNOW
A GREY HAIR...
SO, YOU'VE BEEN SNIVELLIN' ROUND AT YOUR MOTHER'S AGAIN –!
8-19
Smythe

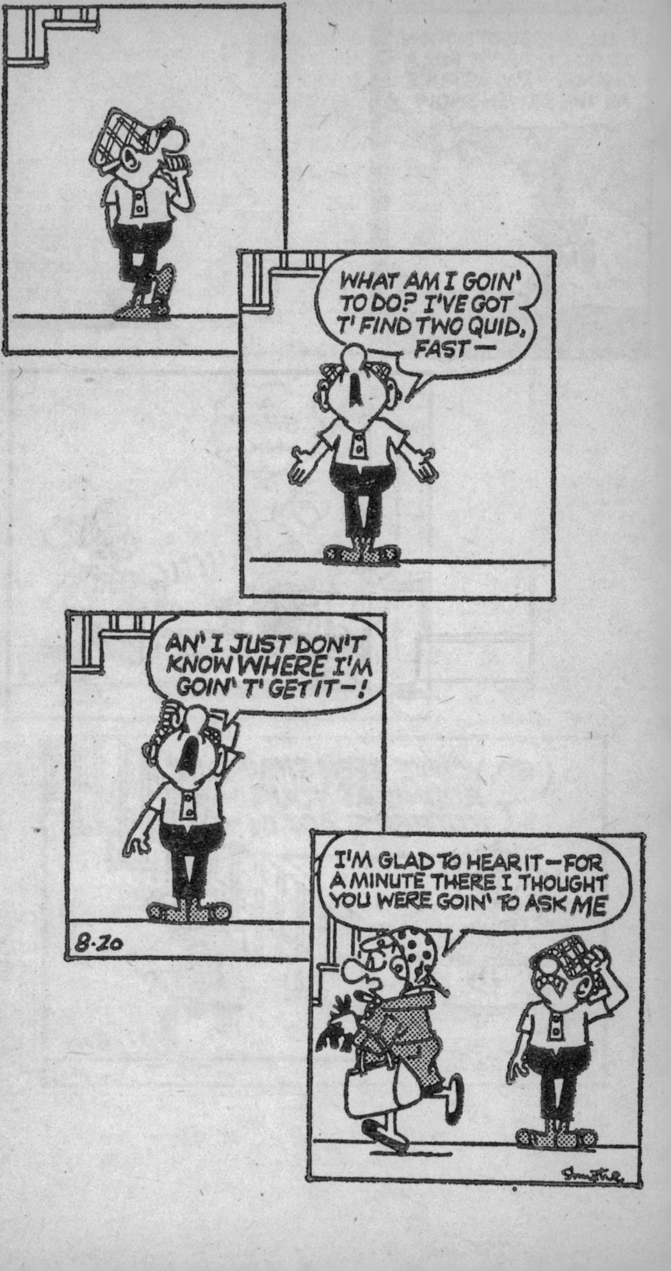
WHAT AM I GOIN' TO DO? I'VE GOT T' FIND TWO QUID, FAST —
AN' I JUST DON'T KNOW WHERE I'M GOIN' T' GET IT — !
8·20
I'M GLAD TO HEAR IT — FOR A MINUTE THERE I THOUGHT YOU WERE GOIN' TO ASK ME

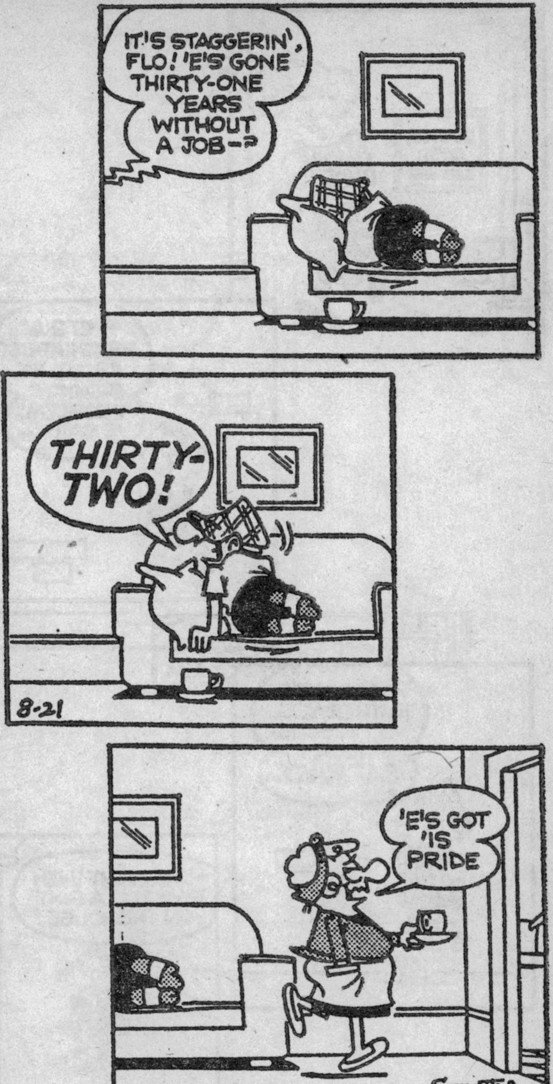
IT'S STAGGERIN', FLO! 'E'S GONE THIRTY-ONE YEARS WITHOUT A JOB--?
THIRTY-TWO!
8-21
'E'S GOT 'IS PRIDE

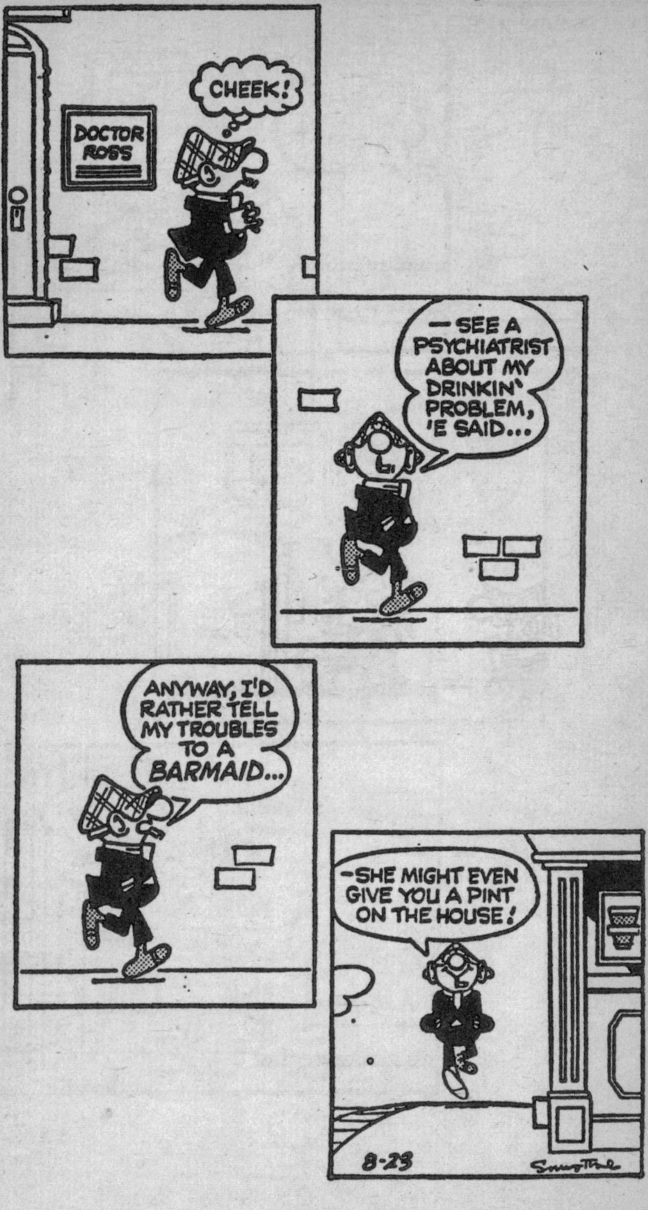
CHEEK!
DOCTOR ROSS
—SEE A PSYCHIATRIST ABOUT MY DRINKIN' PROBLEM, 'E SAID...
ANYWAY, I'D RATHER TELL MY TROUBLES TO A BARMAID...
—SHE MIGHT EVEN GIVE YOU A PINT ON THE HOUSE!
8-23
Smythe

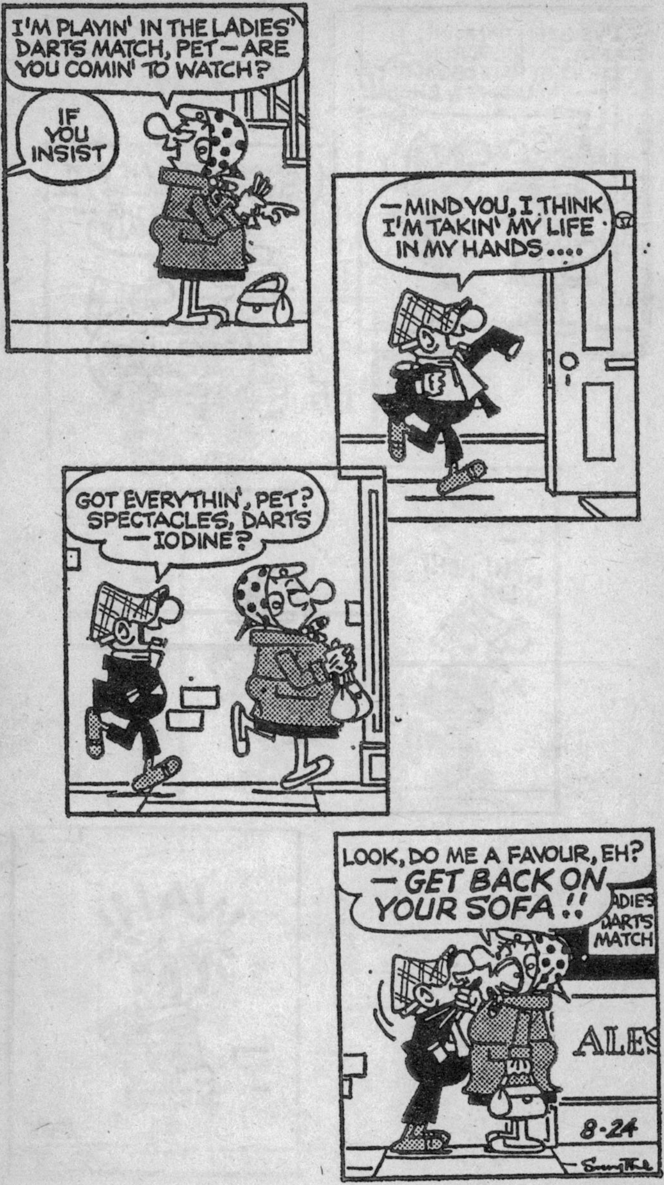
I'M PLAYIN' IN THE LADIES' DARTS MATCH, PET — ARE YOU COMIN' TO WATCH?
IF YOU INSIST
— MIND YOU, I THINK I'M TAKIN' MY LIFE IN MY HANDS....
GOT EVERYTHIN', PET? SPECTACLES, DARTS — IODINE?
LOOK, DO ME A FAVOUR, EH? — GET BACK ON YOUR SOFA!!
LADIES DARTS MATCH
ALES
8-24
Smythe

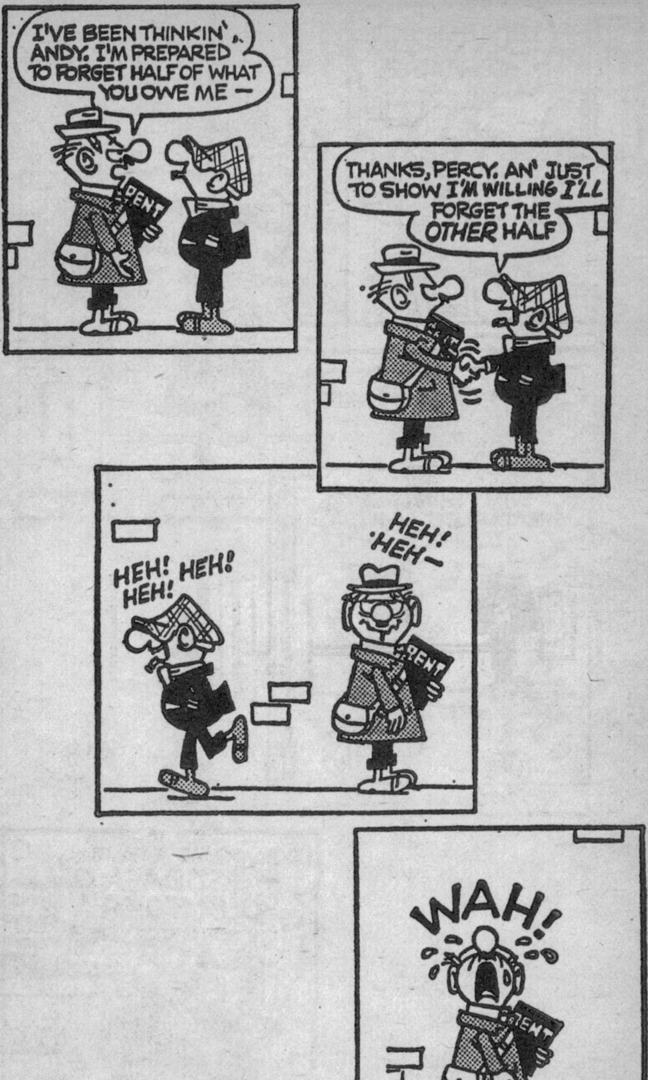
I'VE BEEN THINKIN', ANDY. I'M PREPARED TO FORGET HALF OF WHAT YOU OWE ME —
RENT
THANKS, PERCY. AN' JUST TO SHOW I'M WILLING I'LL FORGET THE OTHER HALF
HEH! HEH! HEH!
HEH! HEH —
RENT
WAH!
RENT
8-25
Smythe

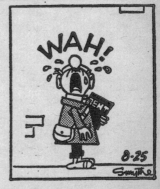

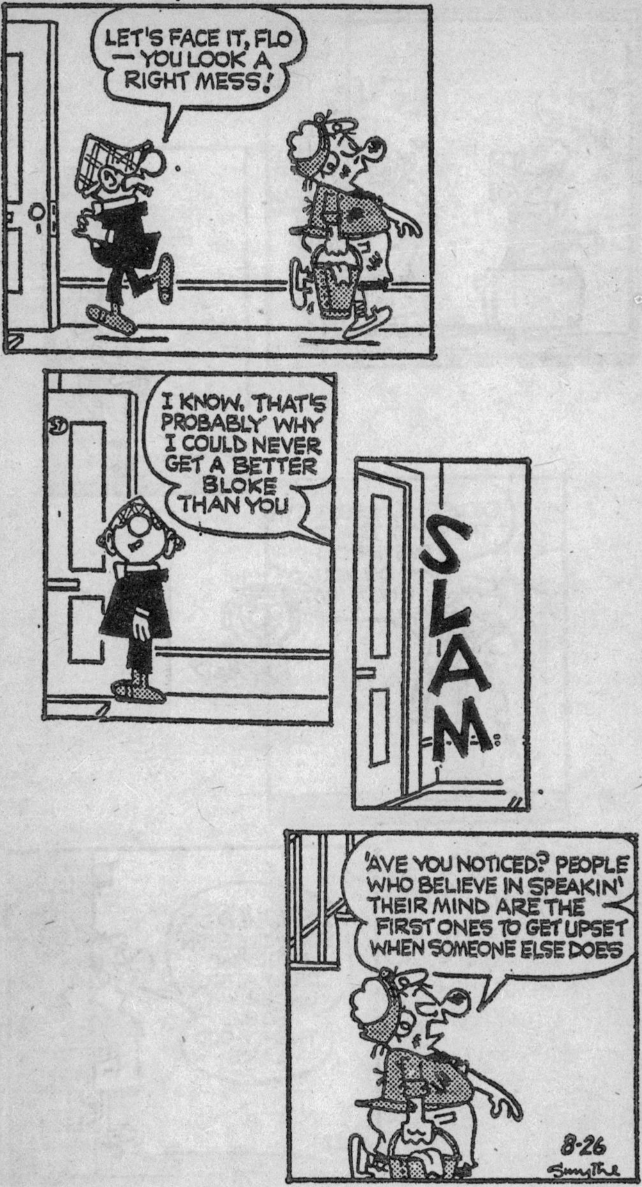
LET'S FACE IT, FLO — YOU LOOK A RIGHT MESS!
I KNOW. THAT'S PROBABLY WHY I COULD NEVER GET A BETTER BLOKE THAN YOU
SLAM
'AVE YOU NOTICED? PEOPLE WHO BELIEVE IN SPEAKIN' THEIR MIND ARE THE FIRST ONES TO GET UPSET WHEN SOMEONE ELSE DOES
8-26
Smythe

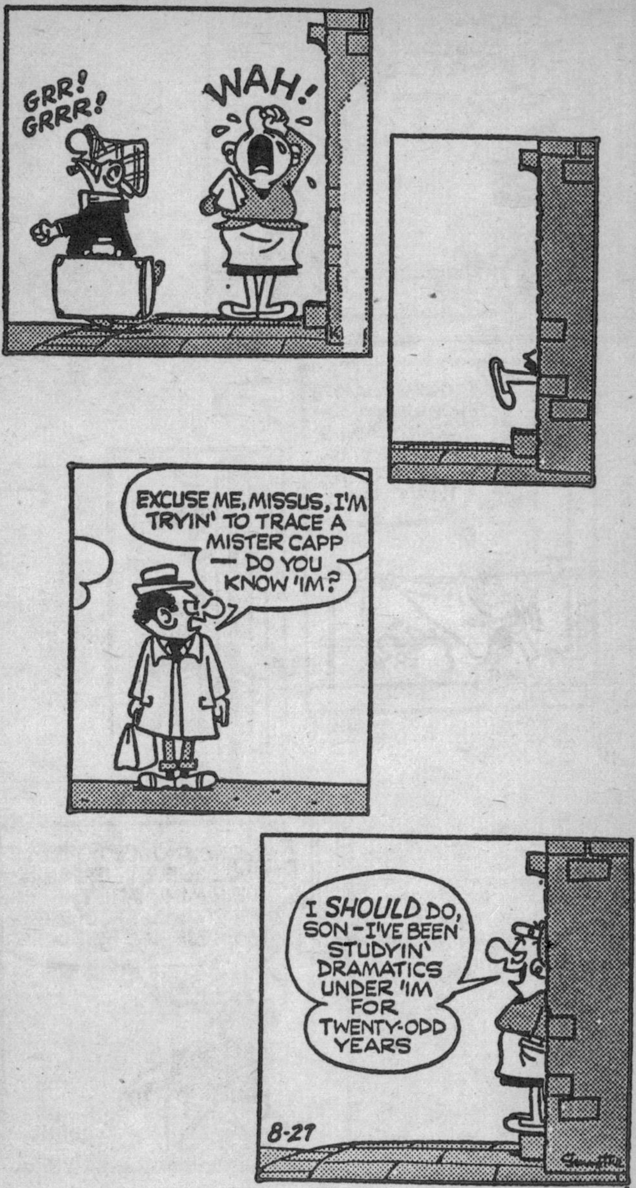
GRR! GRRR!
WAH!
EXCUSE ME, MISSUS, I'M TRYIN' TO TRACE A MISTER CAPP — DO YOU KNOW 'IM?
I SHOULD DO, SON — I'VE BEEN STUDYIN' DRAMATICS UNDER 'IM FOR TWENTY-ODD YEARS
8-27

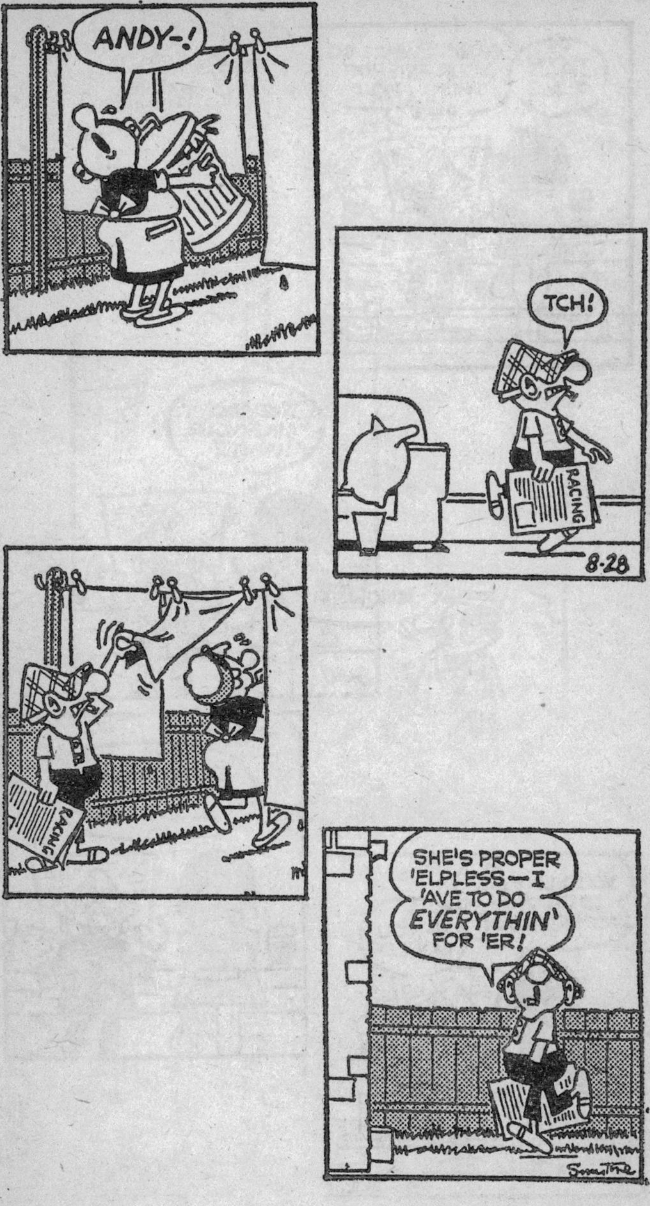
ANDY-!
TCH!
RACING
8-28
RACING
SHE'S PROPER 'ELPLESS—I 'AVE TO DO *EVERYTHIN'* FOR 'ER!

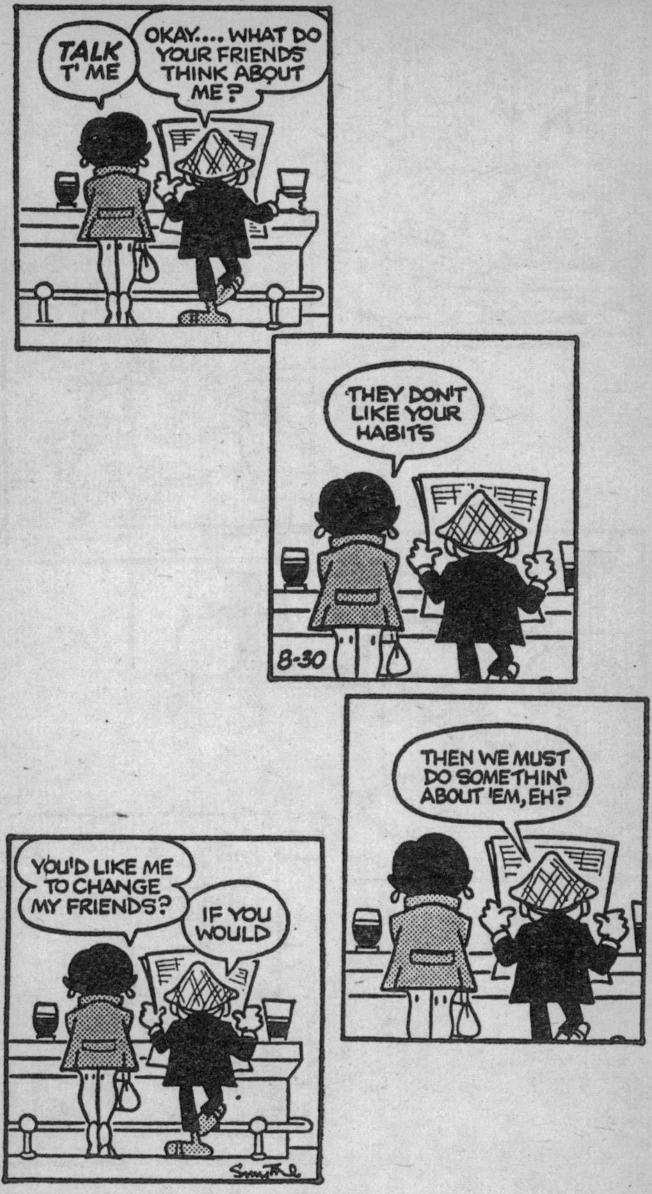
TALK T' ME
OKAY.... WHAT DO YOUR FRIENDS THINK ABOUT ME?
THEY DON'T LIKE YOUR HABITS
8-30
THEN WE MUST DO SOMETHIN' ABOUT 'EM, EH?
YOU'D LIKE ME TO CHANGE MY FRIENDS?
IF YOU WOULD
Smythe

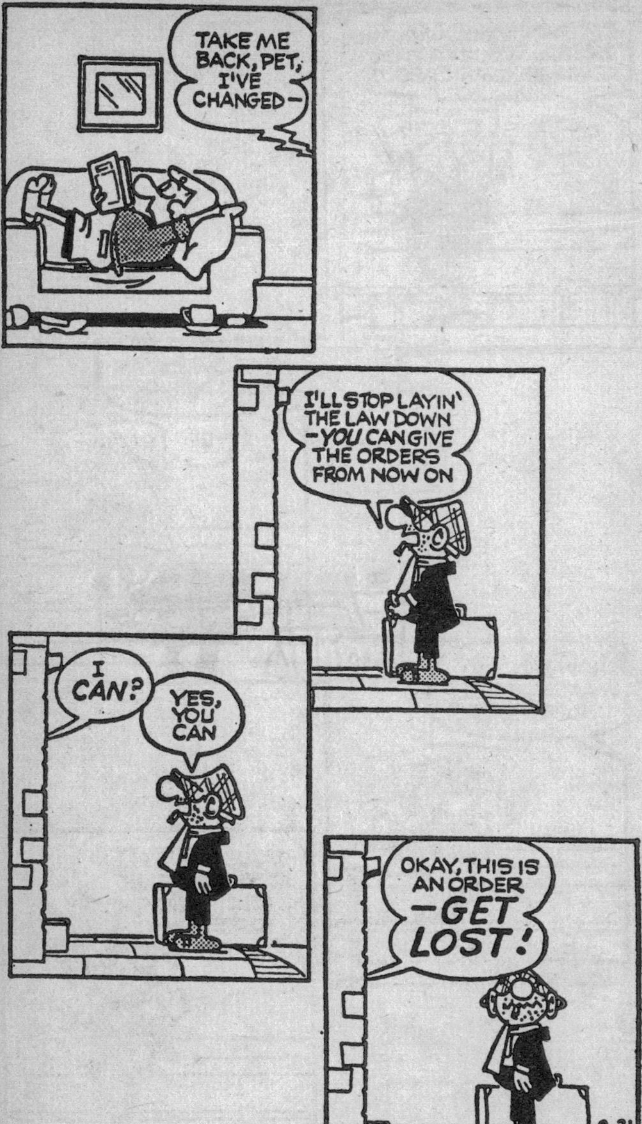
TAKE ME BACK, PET, I'VE CHANGED—
I'LL STOP LAYIN' THE LAW DOWN —YOU CAN GIVE THE ORDERS FROM NOW ON
I CAN?
YES, YOU CAN
OKAY, THIS IS AN ORDER —GET LOST!
8-31

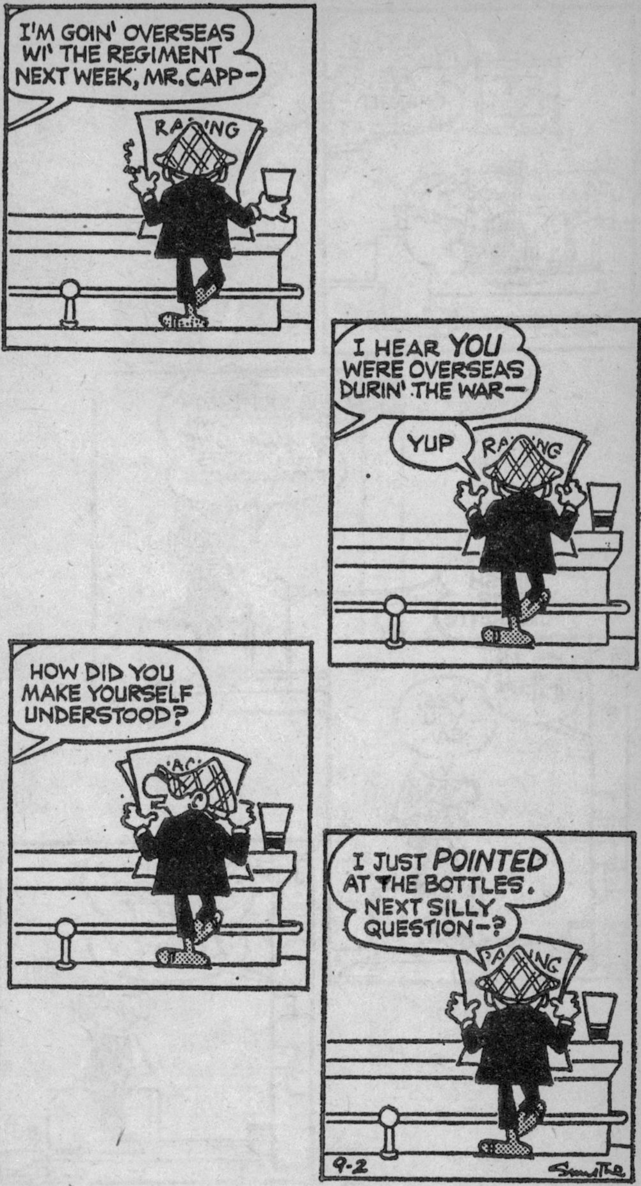
I'M GOIN' OVERSEAS WI' THE REGIMENT NEXT WEEK, MR. CAPP—
I HEAR YOU WERE OVERSEAS DURIN' THE WAR—
YUP
HOW DID YOU MAKE YOURSELF UNDERSTOOD?
I JUST POINTED AT THE BOTTLES. NEXT SILLY QUESTION—?
9-2

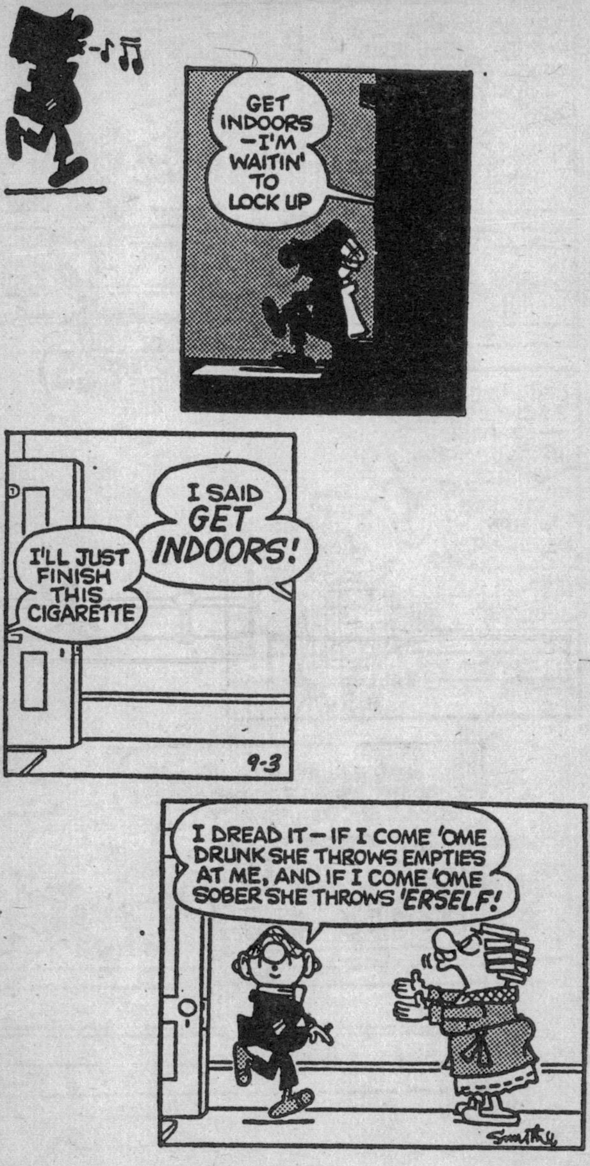
GET INDOORS —I'M WAITIN' TO LOCK UP
I SAID GET INDOORS!
I'LL JUST FINISH THIS CIGARETTE
9-3
I DREAD IT — IF I COME 'OME DRUNK SHE THROWS EMPTIES AT ME, AND IF I COME 'OME SOBER SHE THROWS 'ERSELF!

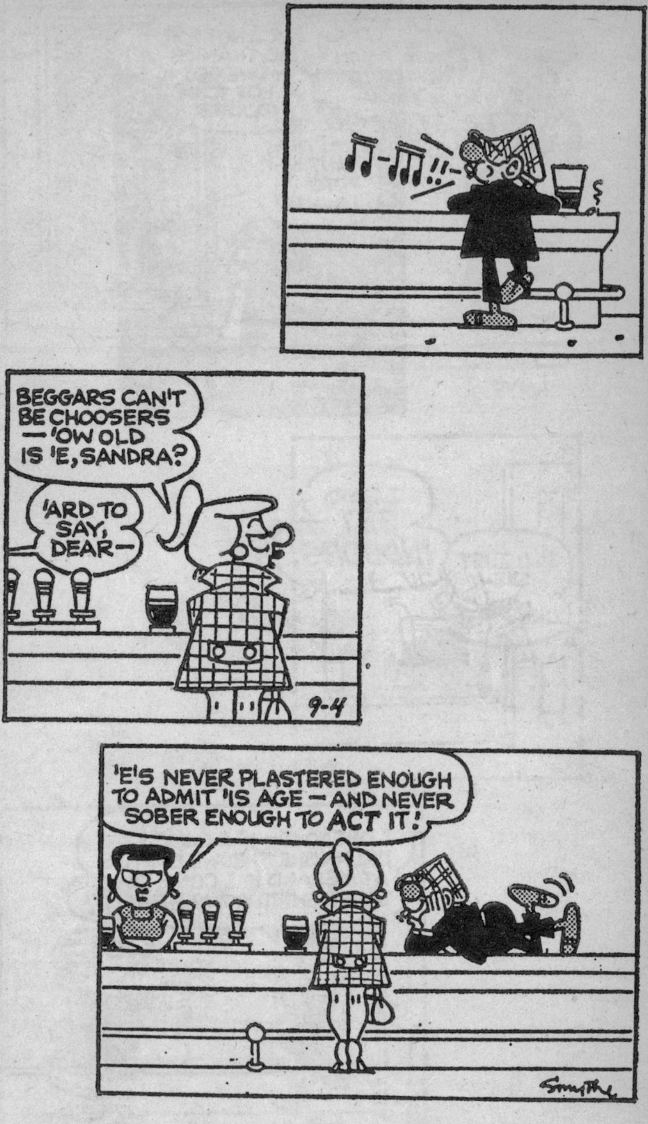
BEGGARS CAN'T BE CHOOSERS —'OW OLD IS 'E, SANDRA?
'ARD TO SAY, DEAR—
9-4
'E'S NEVER PLASTERED ENOUGH TO ADMIT 'IS AGE — AND NEVER SOBER ENOUGH TO ACT IT!
Smythe

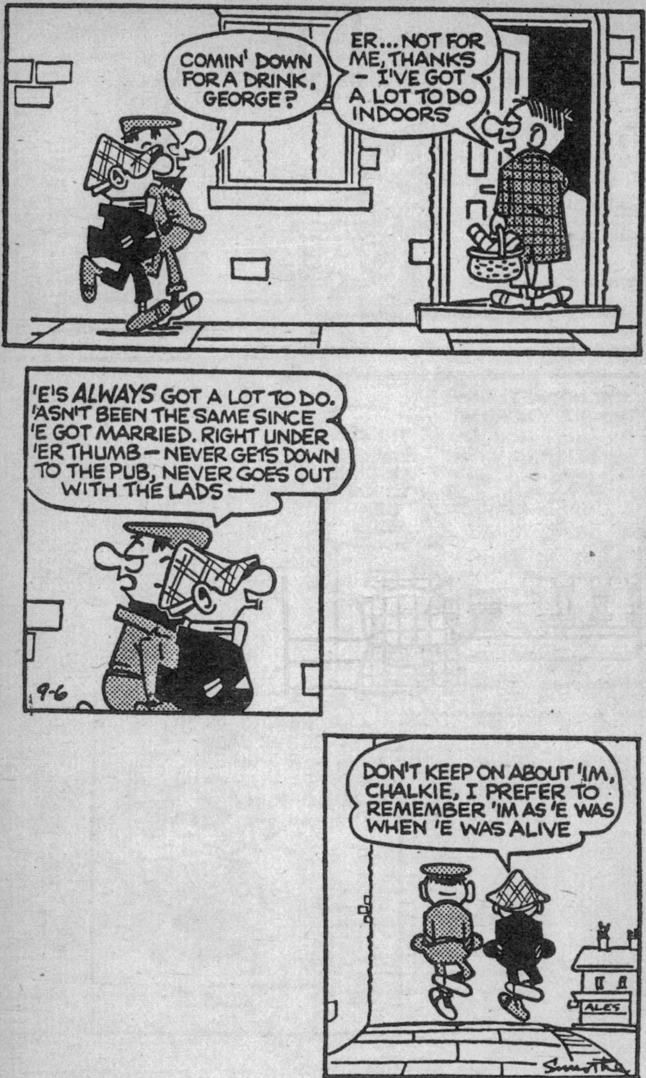
COMIN' DOWN FOR A DRINK, GEORGE?
ER... NOT FOR ME, THANKS – I'VE GOT A LOT TO DO INDOORS
'E'S ALWAYS GOT A LOT TO DO. 'ASN'T BEEN THE SAME SINCE 'E GOT MARRIED. RIGHT UNDER 'ER THUMB — NEVER GETS DOWN TO THE PUB, NEVER GOES OUT WITH THE LADS —
9-6
DON'T KEEP ON ABOUT 'IM, CHALKIE, I PREFER TO REMEMBER 'IM AS 'E WAS WHEN 'E WAS ALIVE
ALES
Smythe

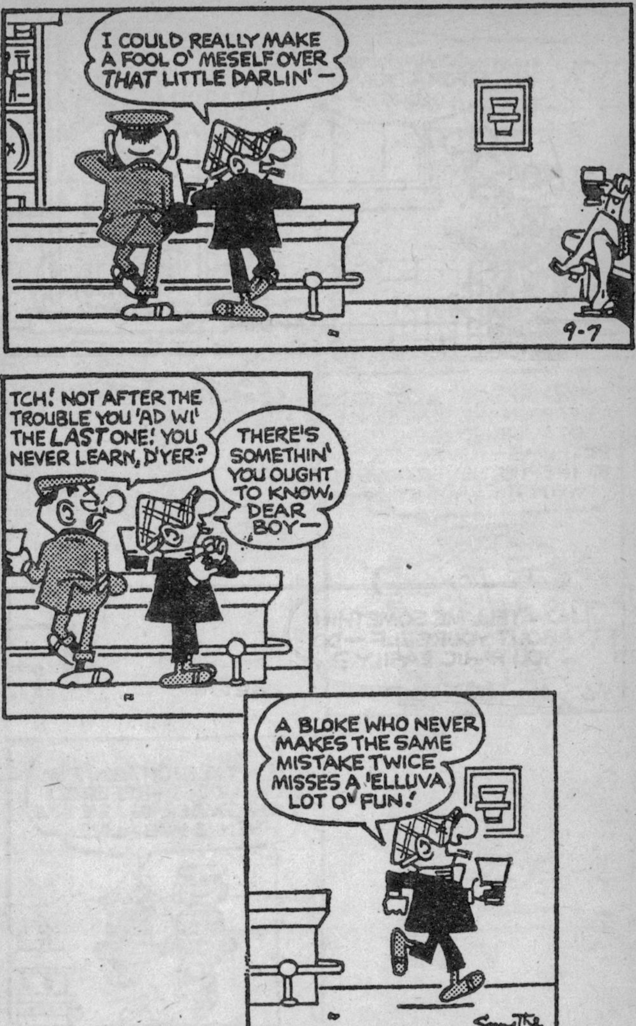
I COULD REALLY MAKE A FOOL O' MESELF OVER THAT LITTLE DARLIN' —
9-7
TCH! NOT AFTER THE TROUBLE YOU 'AD WI' THE LAST ONE! YOU NEVER LEARN, D'YER?
THERE'S SOMETHIN' YOU OUGHT TO KNOW, DEAR BOY —
A BLOKE WHO NEVER MAKES THE SAME MISTAKE TWICE MISSES A 'ELLUVA LOT O' FUN!
Smythe

AN' THAT'S ABOUT ALL THERE IS TO KNOW ABOUT ME
OH-OOH!
YOU'VE BEEN VERY FRANK, MY DEAR
NOW TELL ME SOMETHIN' ABOUT YOURSELF—DO YOU PANIC EASILY?
GRR! GRRR!
9-8
Smythe

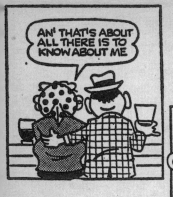

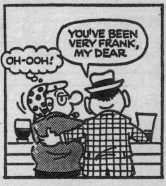

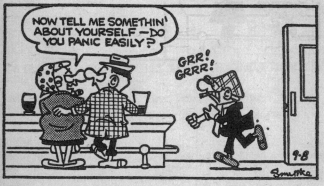

Fawcett Gold Medal Books
in the Andy Capp Series
by Smythe